STUDY AND EXAMINATION TECHNIQUES

Edwin Clough

TEACH YOURSELF BOOKS

Hodder and Stoughton

STUDY AND EXAMINATION TECHNIQUES

This book will help anyone preparing for tests and examinations that include true or false, multiple choice and other short-answer questions, as well as comprehension, problem solving and essay-type questions. The author has wide experience of preparing students for public examinations normally taken at the age of 16+ and 18+, and of helping college students on courses in which the final assessment depends on marks gained in written assignments and progress tests as well as in examinations.

TEACH YOURSELF BOOKS

First published 1986
Second impression 1987

British Library Cataloguing in Publication Data

ISBN 0 340 39146 4

Printed and bound in Great Britain for
Hodder and Stoughton Educational,
a division of Hodder and Stoughton Ltd,
Mill Road, Dunton Green, Sevenoaks, Kent,
by Richard Clay Ltd, Bungay, Suffolk.
Photoset by Rowland Phototypesetting Ltd,
Bury St Edmunds, Suffolk

Contents

Introduction

Why study?

Even if you find all your subjects interesting in themselves, you will still want to do as well as possible in both course work and examinations.

The marks you score in course work help you to know how well you are progressing. Good marks provide encouragement and are a source of satisfaction. Similarly, your grades in examinations are a measure of both ability and achievement.

If you would like to take more advanced examinations or enter a particular career, the grades obtained in your first examinations may fulfil the entrance requirements for the more advanced course or indicate to an employer your interests and achievements. You may study, therefore:

1   to pursue your interest in each of your subjects, and so develop your personality by adding new dimensions to your life;
2   to develop your ability to learn and remember, and to convey your knowledge and understanding in conversation and writing; and
3   to demonstrate to other people your ability to master each subject, by achieving good marks in course work and high grades in examinations.

This book will help you to do these things. It is especially suitable (1) for those aged fifteen to eighteen who are preparing for school-leaving examinations, and (2) for those who have left school and perhaps started upon a career, and are (*a*) taking basic or vocational courses at a local college, or (*b*) taking a correspondence course, or (*c*) teaching themselves solely by private study.

Which subjects should you study?

At first, at school, you studied certain subjects not by choice but because they were part of the curriculum. You probably found some subjects more interesting than others. Perhaps this was because they seemed easy, or you were already interested in them, or you liked the teachers. When you are free to decide, for yourself, which subjects to study, there are a number of things that should be borne in mind:

1   Studying additional subjects may help you to get a broader and more balanced education.
2   If your studies are to be challenging and satisfying you must have a desire to learn, and either study subjects that you find interesting or be determined to develop your interest.
3   You may have to take certain subjects (called pre-requisites), at each stage in your education, to provide a basis for your study of these or related subjects in a more advanced course. Similarly, it may be necessary to study certain subjects before you can start upon a particular career. Therefore, make sure that you study the subjects which are needed to provide a basis for what you plan to do next.
4   You may study part-time, by attending day-release or evening classes or by taking a correspondence course, while you are already engaged in full-time employment. Your employer may encourage you to study certain subjects, or you may choose to study in an attempt to improve your prospects of promotion or change the direction in which your career develops.

Where should you study?

Up to the age of sixteen, whilst at school, the question of where to study does not usually arise. It is normally best, in the years before examinations, to remain at the school at which you started your secondary education so that you can build on the foundations laid by teachers you have known for some years. But if you wish to continue your studies, after taking examinations at the age of 16+, consider where you should do this.

1   Remain at school

You may choose to remain at the same school, with the teachers you know, to prepare for more advanced examinations in subjects selected by yourself but with your teachers' advice.

Consider the choice of subjects that will be possible and whether or not this is satisfactory in relation to what you plan to do after leaving school. Try to find out how successful the teachers at your school have been, in recent years, in preparing students for these more advanced examinations.

2   Continue your studies at a local college

At a local college you may be able to prepare for the same advanced examinations that you would have taken had you stayed at school, but the choice of subjects may be different and you will have different teachers.

These teachers will offer advice on your choice of subjects, based on your performance in your first examinations (taken at 16+) and on your wishes in relation to a particular career or to alternative careers.

If you have failed examinations at 16+ or 18+, or wish to improve your grades, you may prefer to move to a college and to make a fresh start in different surroundings rather than to stay at school and repeat exactly the same course. Different teachers, each with a different approach, may help you to see things in a new light and to do better work.

There will also be vocational courses at a local college, which may not be available at school. These are not necessarily more difficult than courses taken at school but each is designed to prepare people for a particular career.

3   Obtain full-time employment and study part-time

You may decide to start upon a career and to build on the foundation laid at school or college by continuing your education part-time. There may be suitable evening classes at a local college, or your employer may allow day-release so that you can attend a particular course, or you may take a correspondence course.

These methods of continuing your education all have the advantage that you can gain experience and make progress in a career whilst obtaining additional qualifications.

However, a part-time student can devote less time to study than a full-time student and it will probably take longer to obtain qualifications part-time than full-time. Also, after a day's work, considerable determination and self-discipline are required if enough time is to be devoted to study in the evenings and at weekends.

How should you study?

There is little point in studying unless you have a desire to learn, and to do your best work a definite effort is required. Like any other challenging and interesting work, study should be a source of satisfaction and even enjoyment – but it is work. And it needs to be properly organised if as much as possible is to be achieved in the time available.

This book will help you to both organise your work and *improve your study, revision and examination techniques*. Read one chapter at a time early in your course. Chapters 1 and 2 are about learning from class work and from books; and Chapter 3 is about the importance of good time management. Making revision part of study (see Chapter 4), thinking about the kinds of questions set in assessed course work, tests and examinations (Chapters 5 to 8), and learning about revision and examination techniques that other students have found useful (Chapters 9 and 10), will all help you to know what to study, how to organise your studies, and how to communicate your knowledge and understanding in assessed course work, tests and examinations.

Unless you are working entirely by private study, you will also receive comments on your course work and suggestions for improvement from your teachers. Consider their advice carefully, ask questions, and grasp opportunities to discuss your work, so that you can benefit from other people's experience as well as your own.

To do your best work, think not just about the subjects you are studying – understanding, selecting and learning – but also about communicating your knowledge. What is needed to answer a particular question? Select from what you know, plan your answer, present just the information that is required – and score marks!

What materials will you need?

1   Obtain the syllabus for each subject you are thinking of studying (see p. 48) so that you can see what is included.

2 You are advised not to buy notepaper, books, or other materials or equipment until you have had the benefit of your teachers' advice.

3 A good dictionary (see p. 176) is essential for anyone who uses words to convey information and ideas.

How this book will help you

As a result of working through this book, or attending a course on Study and Examination Techniques based on this book, a student should be able to:

1 **understand** how to use a teacher as an aid to learning;

2 **listen** effectively in class or during a broadcast talk;

3 **appreciate** the advantages and disadvantages of distance learning/correspondence courses;

4 **prepare** concise notes, containing the main points of a talk;

5 **appreciate** the importance of working on notes soon after a class to check, clarify, recall and revise;

6 **understand** how to use a textbook as an aid to learning;

7 **know** how to make good use of a library as a source of information and as a place in which to study;

8 **name** the different reading techniques;

9 **read** selectively, using appropriate techniques, and with a questioning mind;

10 **appreciate** the need to keep class notes (supplemented by notes from other sources) in good order for use in further studies;

11 **prepare** a weekly schedule or timetable, including organised classes, and periods for private study and recreation;

12 **list** the conditions needed for effective study in class or elsewhere;

13 **recognise** separate study tasks;

14 **arrange** study tasks in order of priority;

15 **organise** each study session so as to complete one task;

16 **adopt** active study techniques;

17 **concentrate** during each study session;

18 **keep** up to date with course work;

19 **recall** and **revise** as part of study;

20 **know** when and how to ask for help;

21 **appreciate** the need for good English and clear handwriting in all course work and in examinations;

22 **consider** the meaning of each word used in questions set in course work and examinations;

23 **recognise** the different kinds of question set in course work and examinations and know how to tackle them;

24 **appreciate** the importance of setting out the parts of each answer in the same order as in the question, and according to any instructions, to facilitate marking;

25 **appreciate** the importance of each stage in preparing any composition (thinking, planning, writing and checking);

26 **adopt** effective techniques for learning and for revising prior to tests and examinations;

27 **understand** how to score marks in tests;

28 **make** effective use of the limited time available in examinations.

Acknowledgments

The author and publishers are grateful to the following for permission to reproduce short extracts from copyright works: Methuen London Ltd for an extract from *Hopjoy was Here* by Colin Watson (Methuen); Jonathan Cape Ltd, the Executors of the Eric Linklater Estate and A. D. Peters & Co. for an extract from *Private Angelo* by Eric Linklater (Jonathan Cape); Michael Joseph Ltd for extracts from *For Kicks* by Dick Francis (Michael Joseph) and *Gossip from Thrush Green* by Miss Read (Michael Joseph); Lawrence Pollinger Ltd and the Estate of John Masters for an extract from *The Deceivers* by John Masters (Michael Joseph). The extract from *A Reed Shaken by the Wind* by Gavin Maxwell (Longman Green & Co. Ltd, 1957), © The Estate of Gavin Maxwell 1957, is reproduced by permission of Penguin Books Ltd. The extract from *They Have Their Exits* by Airey Neave (Hodder and Stoughton), copyright © 1953 by Airey Neave, is reprinted by permission of Curtis Brown.

PART ONE

Study Techniques

In Part One the advantages and disadvantages of differ- ent methods of study are considered: attending classes full-time, studying part-time, or taking correspondence courses. Advice is then given on basic learning tech- niques: taking notes in class or during broadcast talks, reading and the use of learning resources in a library, making the most of time devoted to private study, and your long-term preparations for tests and examinations.

1

On Course

This chapter will help you to: (1) get the most out of class work at school or college, (2) consider the advantages and disadvantages of working without attending organised classes, and (3) make notes that will provide a sound foundation for your further studies.

Methods of study

In introductory courses, whether you are at school or college full-time, attending evening classes, or receiving postal tuition, much of your work is organised for you. Your teachers or lecturers will have studied the syllabus for your examinations. They will have looked at recent examination papers, similar to those you will be taking. So they should understand what you will need to know; and they can plan courses that are well suited to your immediate needs.

Your teachers, from experience in preparing candidates for the examinations you will be taking, should know how to capture and hold your interest and how to present ideas and information in a way that will help you to understand, learn and remember. They should know which aspects of their subject are likely to prove most difficult for you – and how to help you to overcome these difficulties. But your teachers need your help. And obviously, to gain most benefit from the course, you should do your best to attend all organised classes. See Tables 1.1 and 1.2.

Table 1.1   How a teacher can help you to learn

In a well organised class a teacher can help you to learn by:

1   **Explaining** what the lesson is going to be about, how it follows from your previous work, and why it will help you (for example, by providing a basis for your understanding of further work, or by rounding off an aspect of your studies, or by linking different aspects of your work);

2   **Emphasising** a limited number of main points that you should remember, explaining each one and giving examples;

3   **Providing practice**, if appropriate;

4   **Linking** the main points in an orderly sequence which helps you to understand and leads to a conclusion or to the statement of some general principle;

5   **Recapitulating** by repeating just the main points;

6   **Answering questions**;

7   **Testing** that you have remembered these points, that you have understood them, and perhaps that you can apply your knowledge by answering questions or solving problems; and

8   **Saying** what you will be studying in the next class and what you should do for revision and preparation.

Looking, listening and learning
In an organised class a teacher can help you to learn not only by telling you things and explaining difficult points but also by suggesting how you can help yourself. Teachers can help, for example, by

Table 1.2   Learning from a teacher

Take advantage of opportunities to learn:

1   **Consider** the purpose of the lesson, and write a title in your notebook.

2   **Maintain attention** so that you can note each main point as it is emphasised (perhaps by a word written on a blackboard).
    Listen to any explanation.

3   **Practise** skills.

4   **Recognise** the orderly arrangement of main points, and the connections between them, so that they form a sequence or pattern and can be associated in your memory.
    Appreciate any general principles or conclusions.

5   **Check** that you have appreciated the main points. The teacher's repetition of these points should help you to remember them.

6   **Ask questions**.

7   **Answer questions** to satisfy yourself that you have understood this aspect of the work.

8   **Check** your notes before the next class and consider what you should do for consolidation and preparation.

(1) dictating important definitions for you to write in your notebooks, (2) drawing labelled diagrams for you to copy, (3) asking you to read certain pages in your textbooks, and (4) setting homework that will test or extend your knowledge and understanding. You can

help yourself by attending all organised classes, sitting quietly when the teacher is speaking, listening carefully, making suitable notes, asking questions when necessary, and contributing to discussions.

You should therefore have a notebook or file for each subject – containing notes made as you listen, labelled diagrams, the numbers of relevant pages in textbooks that you were advised to read at different points in your course, and any homework you have completed – which will usually include your teacher's comments and corrections. This notebook builds up into a record of your course work. It is an aid to learning and, before tests and examinations, it is an aid to revision.

Making notes will help you to maintain attention – making it more difficult for your mind to wander. In your notes you capture the teacher's main points and the questions and comments that come to mind as you listen.

One of the benefits of attending classes is that, as in conversation, the things other people say not only inform you but also stimulate your thoughts. Noting such thoughts briefly and quickly, for later consideration, should leave you free to concentrate on what is being said, instead of allowing your mind to dwell upon things said earlier in the talk.

Making notes, therefore, is one technique that will help you to develop your ability to listen – which is essential not only in class work but also in any conversation. Being a good listener is not easy, because it is hard to concentrate on one topic, but to listen carefully is obviously the first step both in understanding what anyone else is saying and in making a relevant reply.

Another difficulty in maintaining attention, apart from being diverted from the speaker's words by your own thoughts, is that you may feel uncomfortable due to unsuitable working conditions or be disturbed by people talking or doing other things. Such distractions break everyone's concentration – and as a result the lesson is not as good as it would otherwise have been.

Lack of attention to class work may be due to a number of factors that affect either your own behaviour or that of other members of the class.

1 *Personal problems*

You may have some personal problem, perhaps not directly connected with study, that is occupying your thoughts. If you do not know what to do, or whom to turn to for advice, ask one of your teachers for help.

2 *Work too demanding*

If you find the work too difficult, you are unlikely to be able to concentrate on things you just do not understand. Either the teacher is not presenting information effectively for you or you do not have the necessary background. You must ask for help from the teacher, or undertake suitable preliminary reading, or perhaps transfer to another course at a level more appropriate to your immediate needs.

3 *Work not demanding enough*

You may find that the work is too easy or that you have covered the same ground already in another class. However, even if you know all the teacher is saying, it is still worth paying careful attention and using the class as an opportunity for revision. You have probably had the experience of seeing a film or television programme twice, and appreciating things in the second showing that you did not see or hear in the first. Most people can benefit from hearing even exactly the same lecture twice (as you might in using a tape recording as a learning aid).

4 *Lesson does not seem relevant*

It is not always easy to accept that your teachers know best what you should study. Why should you spend time on one subject when you really want to study another? Lack of interest in any subject will almost inevitably result in lack of attention. This is why it is important to appreciate the relevance of each of the subjects in your course (see p. viii).

5 *Lack of interest*

If attendance is compulsory, because pupils are required by law to be at school up to a certain age or because day-release and attendance at college is a condition of employment, some members of a class may have little or no interest in study. Unless their teachers can stimulate interest, such reluctant learners may adversely affect the performance of other members of a class whilst gaining little benefit from the course themselves.

However, many of those who start a course reluctantly *do* become interested – either as a result of good teaching or because of a change of heart on their own part. They may then surprise even themselves by the pleasure they find can be derived from study and by their subsequent achievements in assessed course work, tests and examinations, and in a career based upon their studies.

Directly (by their effect on you) and indirectly (if they affect your teachers) any distractions interfere with your listening – and therefore with your learning. This is why it is necessary to maintain order in a class. Similarly, at home when you listen to a broadcast talk it is best if you can do this by yourself – in a room where you will not be distracted by other people doing other things and where conditions are conducive to effective study.

In class you learn from other people as well as from your teacher. For example, you learn from their questions, which you might not have thought of asking, and from the teacher's replies. You can also benefit from talking about your work with other members of the class, and sometimes by asking what they think about aspects of the work that have been on your mind.

If you listen to a broadcast talk in class you can discuss it afterwards. Listening during a talk helps you to understand and remember; and talking about it afterwards may bring your attention to aspects that you might not otherwise have considered. You learn both from sitting quietly during the talk and from the discussion that follows.

The role of the teacher and the learner in class work is summarised in Fig. 1.1. As the learner you not only receive information and ideas, but also show your understanding by expressing your thoughts. That is to say, you should be an active partner: receiving and giving. By observing your reactions, listening to your comments and questions, and marking course work completed in class and for homework, your teachers can monitor your progress. They can modify their teaching to suit the needs of individuals and can respond at once, if anything is not understood, to help you learn.

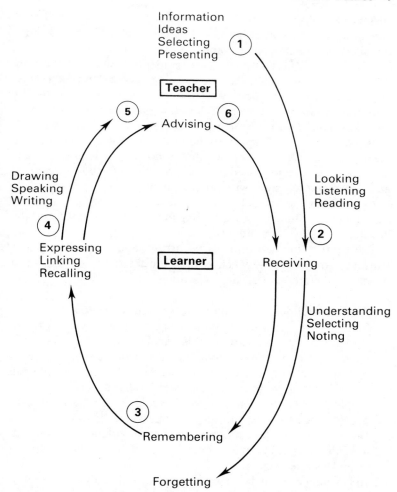

Fig. 1.1 Learning from a teacher. (1) Information selected and presented by the teacher is (2) received by the learner, (3) remembered or forgotten, and (4) may be recalled and expressed in course work, tests and examinations. Assessing course work provides (5) feedback to the teacher, indicating that the work has been remembered, understood and applied successfully, or that it has not. And (6) feedback for the learner, in the form of comments and marks, may provide encouragement and indicate where further work is needed. The learner also receives information in discussions, from personal observations, and from books.

Distance learning

One difficulty about listening to a broadcast at home is that you miss the social stimulation that comes from a good teacher and from discussing the subject with interested students. This is also the main disadvantage of so-called distance learning or postal tuition, involving a written correspondence course that may be supported by sound recordings, radio and television programmes, and other teaching aids. However, in some correspondence courses it is possible for students to speak to their tutors on the telephone, or to meet them at weekend or summer schools which also provide opportunities for supervised practical work and for both organised and informal discussions with other students.

Apart from the lack of social stimulation, isolation can be an advantage to a student – encouraging independent enquiry and the development of self-confidence.

There are other advantages in correspondence courses, as in learning from books – which is the oldest established and most widely used method of distance learning:

1   As with attending a part-time course, you can keep a job and so further your career by obtaining work experience while you are studying for a qualification. This enables you to learn not only from your own employment but also from discussions with colleagues at your place of work, who may be experts either in the subjects you are studying or in related subjects. Your employer may also benefit from these discussions as a result of considering new ideas included in your course of study.

2   Books, and the notes provided in correspondence courses, are available to people everywhere: even to those who could not attend a suitable class.

3   In learning entirely by private study, with no classes to attend, you may be able to devote *more* time to study than would be possible if you attended a part-time course (because no time would be wasted in travelling to and from classes).

4   In reading you can consider each topic as many times as you like, whereas in class some points may be missed as you record others or as your mind wanders for even a short time from the matter in hand.

5   In reading a book, or working on other materials, you can move

quickly through things you already know or find easy to understand but spend more time on anything that seems to be particularly important, or when you encounter some difficulty or have a problem to solve.

6 In a correspondence course your work is planned for you and you receive regular assignments. This ensures that you complete the necessary directed reading and have practice, throughout the course, in answering the kinds of questions set in the tests and examinations you will be taking. You also receive regular feedback in the form of comments on your work, corrections and marks.

Class teaching is not always so well planned, and even with the best intentions a teacher coping with a class of students who vary in their interest and ability may neither succeed in completing a programme of work nor set enough suitable homework assignments.

7 In private study you can arrange to work at times that fit in with other commitments, and you can work in your own room or in a reference library where conditions are conducive to study – with no distractions of the kind that can interfere with learning in a classroom.

Improving your note-taking skills

Take both your textbook and your notebook for the subject with you to each class. Open the notebook and write the date at the top of the next page. When your teacher says what the class is to be about, write a title below the date. Write the name of the teacher unless, after the first class, you have the same teacher for all classes on a particular subject.

Then write any notes neatly, so that you will be able to read them later. At first, in introductory courses, your teachers will probably tell you when to take notes and what to write: your class notes may comprise, largely, what the teacher writes or draws on the blackboard and anything dictated. However, do make additional notes if you think they will be useful when, later, you are making sure you understand this aspect of the work.

Make a note of relevant pages from your textbook, as you look at them in class, so that you can refer to the same pages again if necessary after the class. But do not waste time copying long passages from books. Use your notebook to record the most important points, so that it is an aid to remembering. Use your textbook as a reference book and as an aid to private study. Whenever you study a subject, as you would in class, you should have both your notebook and a textbook for the subject in front of you. Get into the habit of using both.

Soon after a class, devoted to one aspect of your work, you are advised to proceed as follows in your private study.

1   **Survey** your notes to remind yourself of the teacher's purpose.
2   Find answers to your **questions**. How was the material presented? What main points were emphasised in the class? How could each main point be re-worded as a test or examination question?
3   **Read** through your notes carefully to make sure that you do understand them, and add any necessary explanation while the topic is fresh in your mind.
4   Look through these notes, in relation to your earlier work. Select what you consider the most important points and draw attention to them (for example, by underlining or by drawing a line around the words you want to emphasise). Then try to **recall** (recite) these points from memory (with your notebook closed). Write a list or prepare a concise summary, and then check that you have remembered correctly.
5   **Revise** (review) this aspect of your work in a few days' time – perhaps at the weekend.

This sequence in study, which may be remembered as SQ3R – survey (S), question (Q), read (R), recall or recite (R), and then revise or review (R) – is essentially that suggested by F. P. Robinson in 1946 (see his *Effective Study*, Harper & Row, New York, 1970).

If you are unable to make good notes in class, perhaps because you are not yet used to note-taking, it may be necessary to rewrite them after you have made sure that you understand each point, and selected the most important points for emphasis.

However, always try to make good notes in class so that you do not need to rewrite them later, just to make them neater.

Always try to sit near the front in any class. If you have any difficulty in hearing, or in seeing the blackboard or your books, see a doctor without delay.

Writing materials

Unless your teachers ask you to do otherwise, you are advised to use a notebook or loose-leaf file that is A4 size (295 × 210 mm) with wide lines and a 25 mm margin on the left hand side of each sheet, and to use this kind of paper for all your written work.

You may find it helpful to prepare each sheet of paper for note-taking, as in Table 1.3. For example, with A4 paper you will need a space at least 110 mm wide down the centre of each sheet for notes made in class. Therefore, rule a 50 mm margin on the left so that you have space in which to note your own thoughts briefly and to mark anything you do not understand for later consideration. Then leave a margin of up to 60 mm on the right for additions made during your further studies.

Table 1.3 One way to arrange notes during and after a talk

Margin 50 mm wide	Date: Title: Teacher:	Margin up to 60 mm wide
	1 Record Notes made during lesson or broadcast talk. Leave space for corrections and minor additions made during your review after the class.	
2 Question Brief notes of questions and comments that come to mind as you listen to the talk.		**4 Reflect** Space for later additions to your class notes: your own thoughts on the subject; other people's thoughts from discussions or from your further reading.
	3 Reduce After the talk, underline things you wish to remember.	

Exercises

1.1   At the start of your course, after attending the first class, sit quietly and make a list of your reasons for taking this course. What do you hope to achieve by the end of the course? What is your attitude to study going to be, throughout your course?

1.2   Check the notes you made in the first class. Do they include the teacher's main points? Is enough detail recorded? Will you be able to understand them later?

1.3   For practice, use prepared sheets as suggested in Table 1.3 as you make notes during a recorded talk. Check your notes and then listen to the talk a second time to confirm that you have included the most important points.

2

Reading and Learning

This chapter will help you to: (1) choose textbooks that are suited to your needs, (2) make good use of your textbooks, (3) understand the sources of information available in a good library, and (4) ensure that the time you devote to reading is well spent.

Choosing and using a textbook

To do well in examinations you will need a good teacher or a good textbook – and preferably both. A good teacher will explain things and try to make sure that you understand, as a lesson develops, but the teacher must follow a lesson plan so that all that should be said in the lesson can be fitted in to the time available.

In a lesson you have little or no control over the speed of delivery, and in listening to a broadcast talk you have none. You cannot go back to check if you are unsure of something, and you cannot take a few minutes' break if you feel fatigued. Also, some lessons are not as well organised as they might be – and you may not like some teachers or the way they teach.

In learning from a book, however, although you cannot ask questions, you can work at your own pace and take a break if you realise that your concentration has lapsed. Also, you can choose a book that, for you, is both easy to understand and well suited to your needs. See Tables 2.1 and 2.2.

Table 2.1   How an author can help you to learn

An author of a well organised textbook can help you to learn by:

1 **Devoting** each chapter to one aspect of the subject and arranging the chapters in order so that each one builds upon your present knowledge and understanding;

2 **Emphasising** a limited number of main points in each chapter, by using appropriate headings followed by sufficient explanation and examples;

3 **Providing practice** if appropriate;

4 **Linking** the main points by arranging the headings in an orderly sequence which contributes to your understanding and leads to some conclusion;

5 **Summarising** the main points that you should remember;

6 **Testing** your knowledge and understanding, and perhaps your ability to apply your knowledge by answering questions or solving problems;

7 **Stating** how this chapter leads on to the next, and perhaps suggesting further reading that would be appropriate for consolidation and preparation.

Choosing a textbook

Some textbooks are intended for class use, with a teacher to help and guide you, although you may also read them at home. Other books are intended mainly for those who are studying alone – who may be taking a correspondence course or reading in the school holidays or working solely by private study. When choosing a textbook, therefore, look at the *Contents* pages, which indicate its scope, and read the *Preface* or *Introduction* to see if the author considers the book appropriate to your needs and suitable for the

Table 2.2 Learning from a textbook

Take advantage of opportunities to learn:

1 **Survey** the chapter by reading the first paragraph, noting the headings, and reading the summary, so that you can view this aspect of the subject as a whole, see how it is related to your previous work, and understand why it is important for your further understanding of the subject.

2 **Consider** each main point, understand the explanation provided, and if necessary amend the notes you made in class on this aspect of your work.

3 **Complete** any exercises included in this chapter to give you practice.

4 **Appreciate** the orderly sequence of headings, and of paragraphs below each heading, so that the author's arrangement provides a pattern that helps you to associate aspects of your work and so helps you to remember.

5 **Repeat** the main points, from memory, and check that these are included in your notes.

6 **Use** your knowledge and understanding by working through any test questions or solving any problems set in the chapter.

7 **Recall and revise** your work on this chapter, and undertake any further reading necessary to clarify any difficulty so that you are well prepared for reading the next chapter.

kind of examinations you will be taking.

If you are working without a teacher, prefer a textbook that is intended for private study. Such a book will contain more explanation than is necessary in a textbook written for class use, and it should have questions at the end of each chapter – with answers at the end of the book so that you can check your own progress and practise answering the kinds of questions that will be set in your examinations (see Fig. 2.1). With such a book to guide you, start at the beginning and work at your own pace. The first chapter will introduce the subject, the next chapters will deal with fundamentals and help you to increase your knowledge and understanding gradually – until you feel you have mastered the subject and are prepared for the examinations you will be taking.

A book that will help you to teach yourself is also worth having if you want to catch up by private study, and do well in examinations, after falling behind with class work. Or if you do not like the way a subject is presented by a particular teacher or in your class textbook, you may find that a book that helps you to teach yourself puts things in a different way and is both more interesting and easier to understand.

At school you will probably either be provided with a textbook for each subject or asked to buy certain books. But if you have left school and are taking evening classes or attending a local college, you may be given a list of textbooks that are suitable for your course and be advised to select and buy one of them. Before doing so, try to look at each of these books in a library or in a local bookshop. Look at the date of publication (on the back of the title page) to make sure that the book is sufficiently up to date. Remember that a *reprint* or *impression* usually means that no changes have been made, but a *new edition* should indicate when the book was last revised. Read the Preface and Introduction to each book, and the first pages of chapter one, to see if you find each sentence easy to read and understand. Look at the diagrams to see if they help to make things clear. Try to choose a book with which you will feel at ease.

Using a textbook

With a good teacher and a good textbook, your teacher will advise you to read certain pages at appropriate points in your course, and may say that it is not necessary for you to read other pages. This is because the author of a textbook, to cover your needs and those of other students taking similar but not identical courses, may write about topics that are not in the syllabus for the examinations you will be taking.

Your teacher may not teach topics in the same order as they are presented in your textbook for the course, and may recommend you to read certain pages for homework – as preparation before a class or for consolidation after a class. It is always a good idea to read relevant parts of your textbook soon after a class, but this is most important if you are not sure that you understood all that your teacher said. Check in your textbook and then ask the teacher in the next class if there is anything that you still do not understand.

If you are working alone, without the advice of a teacher, or if you find it difficult to learn from a particular teacher for any reason, study the syllabus for the examination you will be taking to see if the topics included in the syllabus are also included in your textbook – and to see if any topics covered in the textbook are additional to your present needs. You can then concentrate, in your reading, on topics that are in your syllabus. This is not to say that you should not read the whole book: if you find the textbook for your course interesting you will probably want to read it all.

Preparing to read
When you first get a textbook, whether it is issued in class or is one that you have borrowed or bought, take it home and spend half an hour trying to understand how the author is trying to help you.

After reading the Preface or Introduction and looking through the Contents pages to see how the subject is developed chapter by chapter, go quickly through the book reading the first and last paragraphs of each chapter.

In later homework periods, when you look at a particular chapter, use a similar approach. Read the first and last paragraphs, and glance through the headings and sub-headings to see what the chapter is about. Then read the last paragraph and the chapter summary. When you have completed this preliminary survey you will have a good idea of the scope of the chapter and will be ready to study the whole chapter carefully, starting at the beginning, or to study just the part that is relevant to your immediate needs.

Understanding and remembering
In your second careful reading, make sure that you understand everything as you go along. For example, the chapter heading and all other headings are signposts that should direct your attention to different parts of the subject. **Bold print** may be used for words that the author would like you to note particularly, to understand, and to remember. Definitions may be printed in *italics*: this again attracts your attention to something you should know. The chapter may end

with a summary to draw your attention, again, to the things the author considers to be most important for your purpose – *which at the moment is to prepare for and to do well in your examinations.*

The words emphasised in headings and sub-headings, and by bold print and italics, are keys to your understanding of the subject. *These are the words that you are most likely to be asked to recall in tests and examinations.* In some questions you will be able to score marks just by writing one word (see p. 83) or by defining a word (see p. 88). In others you will have to write a whole paragraph (see p. 88) or complete a longer composition (see p. 111). In tests and examinations these words, remembered from your textbooks, will remind you of topics that should be included in your answers.

When you feel that you have understood the chapter and can remember the most important points, attempt all the questions at the end. If you can answer them correctly you may feel confident that you have remembered the most important points and understood them. The roles of the author and the reader in teaching and learning from a book are summarised in Fig. 2.1. As the learner you receive information and ideas, consider them, and can test yourself.

Overcoming difficulties
If you are attending classes and there is anything you do not understand, read the appropriate part of your textbook on this subject. If then you still do not understand or you require more information, look at other books or ask a question in class or discuss the problem with your teacher. You will find that most teachers will welcome your interest in their subject.

If you find a chapter in a textbook hard going, at any stage in your studies, perhaps the author has not explained things very well or perhaps you do not have the basic knowledge needed to understand this aspect of your work:

1   Try another textbook to see if this topic is explained in a way that you find easier to understand.
2   Consult a more elementary book, if necessary, to provide yourself with a firmer foundation upon which to build, and then return to your textbook for your course.
3   Use reference books if you have any remaining difficulties.

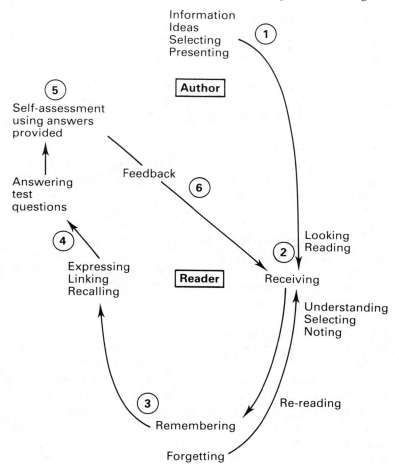

Fig. 2.1 Learning from a book. (1) Information selected and presented by the author is (2) received by the reader, (3) remembered or forgotten, and (4) may be recalled and expressed in answers to test questions included at the end of each chapter in most introductory textbooks. Answers to these questions are also provided, so that (5) self-assessment is possible and (6) the reader can monitor the progress made. Knowledge gained from the book may also be used in answering questions in course work, tests and examinations. Knowledge gained from other sources should also contribute to the student's mastery of the subject (for example, from other books, from discussions and from personal observations).

Making good use of a library

A library is especially important for a student who is working alone, but should also be used as a source of further information by anyone who is seriously interested in study. From library books you will find: an alternative approach to that adopted by the author of your textbook; answers to many of your questions; and sources of further information and suitable background reading.

Studying in a library

It is not a good idea, as some books on study skills recommend, to make a habit of studying always in the same place. You must be able to concentrate *wherever* you are studying – in classes, in your own room, in a library, and in examinations. You are therefore advised to spend some time, each week, working in a library.

By working regularly in a library you can develop your ability to work where others are working. In something like examination conditions you can get used to concentrating on what you are doing while most other people present are working but some are moving about quietly from time to time.

Facilities for study in a library

When you enter any library for the first time it is a good idea to look at the plan, displayed near the entrance, and to tour the library – reading any information panels on the walls, doors and shelves. This will enable you to find out, quickly, what facilities are available and where things that may be useful to you are kept. Also note where there are tables and chairs: some will be intended for people consulting reference books (for short periods) and others for students (who may wish to work undisturbed for several hours).

Asking for help

Remember that the librarians who work behind the reception or enquiry desk not only keep a record of books loaned to readers and receive these books when they are returned, but also answer questions and help people who are having difficulty in finding the information or the book they require.

Borrowing books from a library

Most libraries are open to any students who wish to use reference materials or to study. However, the materials that may be borrowed from the library (e.g. books, tapes and slides) can be taken out only if you have a reader's ticket.

Each book borrowed must be handed to a librarian, so that a record can be kept of its issue, before you take it from the library. And anything borrowed must be returned by the end of the loan period, or sooner if possible, so that it is available again to other library users.

Reference materials you can use in the library

Your library contains a variety of reference materials, in addition to books. For example, there may be maps, photographs, films, video and sound recordings, newspapers and magazines. Reference books are usually kept in a separate quick-reference section, on shelves near the enquiry desk, or in a separate room. There may also be other rooms for particular purposes in the library, or in other parts of a school or college. For example, there may be a map room or a language teaching laboratory. It is up to you to find out where materials relevant to your studies are kept, so that you can make good use of them from the start of your course.

Audio-visual aids

Many libraries have an audio-visual aids section in which facilities are provided for you to study tape-slide programmes, sound and video recordings, and other learning materials. You can use them in your own time, without being disturbed (and you may be able to borrow them for use at home). They are helpful if you have not fully understood something in class, because they give you an opportunity to learn about the same topic from a different teacher who may present information differently or explain things in a way that you find easier to follow. Video recordings and films are particularly useful in providing the kind of information that you may not be able to obtain by personal observation and that cannot be presented in class or in a book.

Books in the reference section of your library

The best way to appreciate the value of a reference section to you in your studies is first to walk around the shelves looking at the kinds of books included, and then to consult books in this section as sources of information frequently during your course.

Reference books include **dictionaries** (some of which define the specialist terms used in your subject – but no others), **directories** (such as telephone directories which contain names and addresses as well as telephone numbers), and **handbooks** (concise reference works dealing with one subject and perhaps including useful data).

However, an **encyclopaedia** is often the first place to look for a concise introduction to a topic, if your textbook does not contain the information you require.

For example, if you were studying biology, geography or physics and came across the term *continental drift*, you might not find it in your textbooks on these subjects. But you could learn from the *Concise Oxford Dictionary* that continental drift is the slow movement of the continents to their present positions on a deep-lying plastic substratum. And you could learn from the *Encyclopaedia Britannica* that the hypothesis that continental drift has occurred was proposed by Francis Bacon in 1620, and supported forcefully by Alfred Wegener in 1912 when this radically new interpretation of Earth history aroused international interest and violent controversy, but Wegener's hypothesis was supported by studies of Earth's magnetism in the 1950s and a modified version of his theory is now generally accepted.

Books for reference and for borrowing

The subject index

To find where books on a particular subject are kept in your library, look first at the subject index. This alphabetical list may be a card index, with a separate card for each entry (see Table 2.3), or it may be a computer print-out.

Note that books on any one subject are not necessarily kept in one place: the librarian has to decide where to put them so that each book is most readily available to those readers who are most likely to need it.

Table 2.3 Some words beginning with the letter C from the subject index of a library

Dewey number	Subject Index Listing
917.94	California: Geography
910.144	California: Water Resources: Economic Geography
979.404	California: 19th Century History
745.6	Calligraphy
778.5349	Cameras: Amateur Cinematography
771.3	Cameras: Photography
796.54	Camping

The words included in the subject index refer to aspects of the subject. From these you select words that are most likely to take you directly to books containing the information you require. The numbers next to these words (see Table 2.3) are those marked on the shelves, where books marked with these same numbers are shelved.

See Table 2.4 for an introduction to three systems for marking books and shelves, used in different libraries, to help librarians to keep books on each subject together as far as possible and to help readers to find a particular book or to browse through books on a particular subject.

The classified catalogue

To see books on a particular subject you could go straight to the shelves marked with the numbers you had selected from the subject index (for example, 375.4284 Study skills: Higher Education; and Study Techniques: Schools) and there you should be able to find any books on this subject that are in stock – if they are neither out on loan nor being used in the library.

To find out which books are in stock on this subject, including those that are not on the shelves because they are being used by other readers, you would have to look at the classified catalogue. In this list, books are arranged in the same order as on the shelves. That is to say they are in numerical order according to subject (see Table 2.5), and then all books with the same number are arranged alphabetically according to the author's name (as in Table 2.5).

Table 2.4   Key to some numbers and letters used in catalogues, in the subject index, and on the books and shelves of libraries*

| | Classification Systems | | |
| | | | |
SUBJECT	Dewey Decimal System	Universal Decimal System	Library of Congress System
General	000	0	A
Reference		030	03	AE
Journalism		070	07	PN
Philosophy	100	1	B
Psychology		150	15	BF
Religion	200	2	BL
Social Sciences	300	3	H
Politics		320	32	J
Economics		330	33	HB
Law		340	34	K
Education		370	37	L
Commerce		380	38	HD
Languages	400	4	P
Pure Sciences	500	5	Q
Mathematics		510	51	QA
Astronomy		520	52	QB
Physics		530	53	QC
Chemistry		540	54	QD
Biology		570	57 to 59	QH to QR
Applied Sciences	600	6	
Medicine		610	61	R
Agriculture		630	63	S
Business		658	658	HF
Marketing		659	658.8	HF
The Arts	700	7	N
Photography		770	77	TR
Music		780	78	M
Literature	800	8	P
Geography		910	91	G
Biography		920	92	CT
History		930	93	C

* See the list displayed in your own library.

Table 2.5 Some books on study selected from the Classified Catalogue of a library

Dewey number	Book title and author Place of publication, publisher and date
371.302812	*Starting to Teach Study Skills* / Irving A. London, Edward Arnold, 1982 3rd Ed.
371.302812	*Psychology of Study* / Mace C. A. Harmondsworth, Penguin, 1969 Rev. Ed.
375.4284	*Reading Skills: a guide for better reading* / Adams, W. R. New York, Wiley, 1974
375.4284	*Critical Reading* / King M. L. Ellinger B. D. Wolf W. Philadelphia PA, Lippincott, 1967
375.4284	*Print and Prejudice* / Zimet S. G. Hoffman M. London, Hodder & Stoughton, 1976

The author or name/title catalogue

If you are looking for a particular book (or audio-visual aid) and you know the name of the author or the title, look at the author or name/title catalogue. This may be a card index, with a separate card for each book in the library, or details of many books may be included (in alphabetical order according to the name of the author and the title of the book) in very small letters on blue-tinted acetate sheets. To see the entries on these sheets a microfiche reader must be used: this projects a magnified image on a ground glass screen.

Table 2.6 Some entries in the author or name/title catalogue of a library

ALLEN, W. (1981)
    Short Story in English
    Oxford, Clarendon Press
    Shelved at 809.31   A44

ARYA, A. P. (1974)
    Elementary Modern Physics
    Mass, Addison-Wesley
    Shelved at 530.   A79

ASTRONOMY
    Frederick L. W.   Baker R. H.
    New York, Van Nostrand, 1976   10th Ed.
    Shelved at 520   F72

The acetate sheets are stored in a folder next to the reader. After selecting a sheet it has to be placed in position below a lens, focused so that it can be read, and then moved by hand from column to column to find the entry for the book that interests you. Complete bibliographic details are given for each book (as on an index card, see Table 2.6): the name of the author, the date the book was published, the title of the book and the sub-title if there is one, the place of publication and the name of the publisher, and the book number to indicate where the book is kept in the library. Publications of an organisation, if these do not have an author, may be included in this catalogue under the name of the organisation.

Reserving a book
The book you require may be in the catalogue yet not on the shelf, because another reader is using it. The librarian can tell you if the book is on loan and will show you how to reserve it for your use.

Books in other libraries
The book you require may not be in stock in your library. To find if this book is still in print or the date of the latest edition now in print, and to find the name of the publisher and place of publication, consult *Books in Print* (published in New York) and *British Books in Print* (published in London), in the reference section of your library. By looking up either the name of the author or the title of the book, you can find complete bibliographic details (see Table 2.6) of any book published in the United States of America or in Britain that is still in print. Given this information, your librarian may be able to borrow the book for you from another library or tell you if it is in stock in another convenient library.

Improving your reading skills

In study rapid reading is not necessary, and in some circumstances is undesirable. It is more important that you should read carefully, making sure that you take the right meaning. However, very slow reading can be a handicap in everyday life, in study, and in many professions. Consider, therefore, whether or not you should try to increase your reading speed.

Reading faster

Some readers mouth words, as they read them, even though they do not say them aloud. This makes it impossible for them to read faster than they can speak. Therefore, check that you do not mouth words when you are reading.

Some people, as they read, keep glancing back to words already seen. To make sure you do not do this, consciously move forward and try to get into the habit of making your eyes move quickly so that you learn to take in phrases rather than single words: let your eyes pause at perhaps three places on each line of print rather than on every word.

Some readers are held up or they take the wrong meaning because they do not understand certain words. Therefore, learn the words of each of your subjects as you come across them – and make sure that you know exactly what each one means. Also, consult a dictionary if you are unsure of the meaning of any word.

Reading for pleasure

In reading well written articles and books, by successful authors: (*a*) you see the world through the eyes of others and learn from their experiences as well as from your own, and (*b*) you appreciate, even if sub-consciously, how other people express their thoughts. Without attempting to copy anyone else's style, (*c*) your ability to express yourself improves, (*d*) your vocabulary expands, and (*e*) your reading speed increases.

Reading according to your purpose

Some people know of only one way to read a book – by starting at the beginning and reading every word on every page. However, this is time-consuming and is not usually necessary. In study, more time is wasted by reading too much than by reading too slowly. Therefore, before you start to read a book, always consider: what information you require, why you are looking at this book, and how you should use it.

Skim-reading

Look through *this* book, skim-reading, if you have not done so already. Read the headings and sub-headings on the *Contents* pages so that you are aware of the scope of the book and can see what each chapter is about. Read quickly through the *Introduction*.

If you had to prepare for a test made up of multiple choice questions, which part of this book would you read? You may note from the Contents pages that Chapter 5 includes a section on multiple choice questions.

If you had to write an essay, on which pages of this book would you expect to find advice? It is a good idea to look at the *Index* so that your attention is drawn to all pages that are likely to be useful for a particular purpose.

In the *Index*, look at the entries:

> Essays,
> > planning
> > writing
> Multiple choice questions
> Multiple response questions

and then turn to these pages. You do not need to read every word. Just let your eyes skim the pages: get an idea of what each paragraph is about.

Skim-reading selected pages should help you to decide how to use this book. You were advised, in the Introduction, to read the whole book early in your course. But you can also use it as a reference book. Whenever you need help with your studies, the Contents pages and Index should enable you to go straight to relevant pages.

Scan-reading

Scan pages when you are looking for particular words (key words such as are used in the index), so that you can find quickly the chapter, section, paragraph, and so the sentence containing the information you require.

In scanning, let your eyes pass quickly over the page. The author, especially in a textbook, may draw your attention to key words, to help you in your search, by including them in headings, or by emphasising them in **bold** or *italic* print, and by indicating in the first words of each paragraph what the paragraph is about.

Scan when you know what you are looking for. Having found a book which, judging from its title and sub-title, may contain the information you require, look at the contents pages to see if there is a relevant chapter or section heading – so that you can go directly to the few pages that are likely to be of most interest.

When you have looked at these pages, especially if you have found them helpful, look up the same key words in the index. You may find further relevant information in other parts of the book. Scanning is made easy in the index because the words are in alphabetical order and you should be able to go directly to the key words. Remember, however, that for most words there are synonyms or words that are very similar in meaning: if you cannot find one word in the index you may find a synonym.

Consult the index if the contents pages do not help you to go directly to a particular section of the book. Authors try to concentrate information on one topic in one place and to make this clear on the contents pages, but this is not always possible. In this book, for example, advice on preparing for examinations is mainly in Chapter 10, but if you wanted to know how to tackle a particular type of question you would find advice in one of the chapters 5 to 8, and advice on your long-term preparations for examinations is mainly in Chapter 4.

Study-reading

Having found the pages of a book that are of immediate interest, for example in the section of your textbook that deals with a particular aspect of your course, read them carefully – making sure that you understand every sentence, formula or calculation.

It is usually best to read such important passages quickly to see what is included, how the material is arranged, whether or not any conclusion is drawn, and whether or not there is a summary of main points. Then work through the passage in a second, more careful reading in which you confirm that you do understand, recognising steps in any argument, and perhaps making notes for future reference.

You should not, in reading, simply absorb an author's words so that information passes from mind to mind without thought on your part. In an introductory course you have to rely on your teacher to recommend a good textbook which is appropriate for the course you are taking, but as a scholar you must learn to read these or any other books critically. Unfortunately, but perhaps inevitably, books do contain mistakes and it is as well to check in other books if you think that anything you are reading may be incorrect. For example, the book may say one thing and your teacher may say another.

Also, as a scholar you should learn to distinguish opinion from evidence, to detect if an author is biased for or against a point of view, and to recognise when only one side of an argument is being presented.

When reading your textbooks you may just note a page number at the most appropriate place in your class notes, or you may modify these notes in the light of your additional knowledge and better understanding. Similarly, when you are reading any other publication you may wish to add to your notes.

Making notes as you read

At the very least, whenever you read, keep a note of the source of any information (author, date of publication, title, etc., set out as in Table 2.6). With such complete bibliographic details, and a note of relevant page numbers, you will be able to find the same paragraphs again if you need them.

Making notes as an aid to concentration

In reading (as in listening, see p. 6), making notes will help you to maintain attention – provided that you note only selected headings, key words and definitions. If you find yourself copying whole sentences and paragraphs you will usually be writing too much.

After making notes, as a further aid to concentration and to check that you have a record of the most important points, consider if there is anything you should add to your earlier class notes on this topic. Alternatively, you may have your study notes open, whenever you read, so that if necessary you can make minor additions or corrections.

It is important that your notes should be an aid to active study. If they contain more information than you need to help you prepare for your examinations, they will probably be less useful for revision than would more concise notes. Similarly, if your notes contain many pages photocopied from books, these will probably contain more detail than you need. It is best to refer to books at relevant times in your course, and to incorporate in your own notes just the points that are important for your purpose.

Skim-reading and scanning will help you to find, quickly, the parts of a book that are of immediate interest. The SQ3R sequence in study, recommended on p. 12 for use when working on your own notes after a class, can then be applied in your study reading: (1) **Survey** the chapter or paragraphs containing the information you require. (2) **Question**: What do I need to know? What are the author's main points? How might these be re-worded as test (quiz) or examination questions? (3) **Read** relevant parts carefully, section by section, noting the main points. (4) Check your notes, considering the points you have selected as being particularly important: then try to **recall** (recite) these main points from memory by preparing a list or summary. (5) **Revise** (review) this work on the next day: this need not take long. See Table 2.2 (p. 17).

Summary writing as an aid to learning
Most introductory textbooks include chapter summaries, and questions to test that you have understood and remembered the most important points. After reading part of your textbook it is a good idea to try to list the points you wish to remember, or to prepare your own summary – including only the topic of each paragraph or perhaps only the main point of each section. You can then compare your summary with the author's.

Précis writing as an aid to study
Whereas a summary includes only the author's main points, a précis includes all essentials. Writing a précis of an important passage, therefore, makes you read carefully and exercise judgment – as you select essentials and omit supporting examples, figurative language and any superfluous words.

Practice in précis writing will also help you to concentrate on essentials in your own writing, leave out words and sentences that are not working for you, and develop a more direct and forceful style.

Exercises
2.1   Check, as suggested on p. 18, that each of your textbooks is suitable for the course you are taking, is the latest edition, and is interesting and easy to read.
2.2   Get to know your textbooks, as suggested on p. 19.

2.3 Get to know what facilities are available in your library, as suggested on p. 23. Look at the subject index, and at the classified and name/author catalogues, to make sure that you know how to use them to help you find the information you need.

2.4 Get into the habit of skim-reading to help you decide if any article or book is worth reading, or to help you get an idea of the whole before you begin to study selected parts.

2.5 Read the five paragraphs following the heading *Reading and Learning* below. Then: (1) make concise notes of the author's main points, (2) prepare a summary including these main points, and (3) write a précis of the same passage. Your summary and précis should be in good English, not in note form.

Reading and learning

Anyone who can read, who has access to a good library, can learn from good teachers. That is to say, a library is in itself a university. Starting with an introductory textbook, it is possible to study any subject from the beginning and to find books suited to your needs until you are exploring the frontiers of knowledge.

Those who read widely soon come across differences of opinion, see how evidence can be interpreted in different ways, and learn to detect biased judgment – based on pre-conceived ideas more than upon things as they are. They may read one side of an argument in one book, another side in a second, and several sides in a third. Read, therefore, as Francis Bacon (1561–1626) advised in his essay *Of Studies*: 'not to contradict and confute, nor to find talk and discourse, but to weigh and consider'.

Bacon also advised the student that 'some books are to be read only in parts; others to be read but not curiously; and some few to be read wholly, and with diligence and attention'. Remember this advice and adopt reading techniques that are appropriate to the book in your hand and to your purpose. Usually, as a student, you will be seeking information on a particular point or reading for ideas. But you may also read for pleasure, and as an aid to relaxation, enjoying well chosen words, the smooth flow of language, and a story well told.

In reading well-written books you see words chosen carefully, spelt correctly and arranged in effective sentences – with each sentence conveying a whole thought or a few closely related thoughts. You see sentences arranged in paragraphs and paragraphs arranged in an effective order – with each word, sentence and paragraph helping the writer to convey thoughts and to lead the reader on.

As you consider how other people write you will also learn to criticise your own compositions. Your own use of language will improve. You will be better able to explain, convince or persuade. In short, you will find it easier to get your own way!

Comments on Exercise 2.5

Complete your notes, summary and précis; then compare them with the specimen answers below. Are your notes satisfactory? Does your summary include only the main points? Does your précis contain any unnecessary words? See also pp. 102–7 and p. 137.

Specimen answers

Reading and learning

Notes

Reading – key to knowledge
You also learn: to read according to your purpose,
to read critically,
to use words more effectively.

Summary

Books are keys to knowledge, and people who read widely soon learn to read critically, to match their method of reading to their immediate needs, and to improve their own use of words – so that they are better able to explain, convince or persuade.

Précis

In a good library any reader can begin with an introductory textbook and continue to the boundaries of knowledge. People who read widely soon learn to recognise differences of opinion and to detect biased judgments. In reading, therefore, follow the advice of Francis Bacon: read critically, do not just disagree or accept without thought, and read each book according to both its merits and your purpose.

You may read to find information or ideas, or solely for pleasure, but in reading any well-written book your own use of language improves. Seeing words used effectively helps you to influence your readers – to explain, convince or persuade – so that you achieve your purpose in any composition.

3

Teaching Yourself

This chapter will help you to: (1) devote enough time to study, recreation and sleep, (2) decide when to study and what to do in each private study period, (3) concentrate when you are working, and (4) adopt an active approach to learning.

By deciding which points to note as you listen to a talk, and by reviewing your notes afterwards, and then by working on them in your further studies – you make them your own. In this way, in preparing for tests and examinations, you accept more and more responsibility for your learning. You rely more and more on your own judgment. Instead of being a *pupil*, learning just what you are told, you are a *student* – recognising gaps in your knowledge and understanding, deciding what needs to be done to fill these gaps, and then teaching yourself.

Keeping up to date with set work

Try to attend to each piece of homework soon after it is set. Obviously you must do so if the work has to be handed in on the next day for marking.

Tackling homework while class work is fresh in your mind should make it easier. Thinking about the work again, soon after you first thought about it, will also help you to remember the most important points – and some of the details.

Organising each study session

Most tasks set for homework are based on what you have been doing in class. You will usually be able to complete each task in 30 to 50 minutes; and you should therefore be able to do homework in two or three subjects in one evening of properly organised study.

However, you may sometimes be asked to do things that will take more than one hour. Then, even if you are given more time to complete the work, it is still advisable to make an early start. Plan how you will divide the work into short study sessions. For example, you may be set an essay and asked to complete it in one week. You might then spend 15 minutes on the first evening just thinking about the title, considering what it means, and noting topics that might be included in your composition (see p. 125). On another evening you could spend 15 minutes looking at your textbook or class notes to refresh your memory and to see if there are other topics that should be considered for inclusion. On a third evening you could think again about your notes for the essay and spend 15 minutes preparing a plan for your composition (see p. 129). Then on a fourth evening, or perhaps at the weekend, you could reconsider your plan as a basis for an answer to the question asked, and then write your answer (using your plan as a guide, see p. 132). You should be able to do this in 30 minutes – which is as much time as you would have in an examination for thinking, planning, writing a complete answer, and checking your work. On another day you could read through your work to check that it is complete, that it reads well, and that it contains no slips of the pen or other obvious mistakes (see p. 139).

If you have homework in more than one subject in an evening, try to complete each piece of work in less than an hour. Within each task, recognise smaller tasks. For example, if asked to read certain pages in your textbook, you might spend 30 minutes **reading** (see p. 31), 20 minutes making notes (see p. 32), 5 minutes **recalling** what you have learnt and preparing a summary (see p. 33) and then, for **revision**, 5 minutes listing the main points from memory and checking this list to ensure that it includes all the points that you wish to remember (see Table 3.1).

If you plan to work at just one subject in an evening, you may complete a piece of written work in the first hour and then spend another two hours reading, reflecting and making notes. You may find that you achieve more by doing this than by switching from

Table 3.1   Making yourself think: allocating your time to different activities in an hour devoted to one study task

Consider	*Note*	**Recall**	**Revise**
Survey	Select	Recall	Remember
Question	and	and	Summarise
Read	record	reconsider	Check
30 minutes	*20 minutes*	*5 minutes*	*5 minutes*

subject to subject. In other words, *there is no need to treat every study session in the same way*. On some evenings you may study just one subject, and on others two or three. With experience *you will find study routines that fit into your timetable and suit you best*.

Working for yourself

If you have set homework, decide when you will do it and then attend to it in this time. If you really want to master your subjects and do well in tests and examinations, make study your top priority – and then fit other things in to your free time. Do not put other things first in the hope that there will be time for you to catch up with your studies later. That way, you would probably find insufficient spare time and your studies would be neglected.

In doing homework you are not working for your teachers but for yourself. In attending classes and doing homework on the same subjects you learn more and more. You increase both your knowledge and understanding. Attempting to score good marks for all set work provides you with short-term goals. The good marks obtained, like praise for work well done, provide encouragement and are a spur to further effort that will help you to achieve your long-term goal. Each lesson attended and each exercise completed should be appreciated as an end in itself and as a step towards success in your tests and examinations.

If you are attending school or college (full-time or part-time), all that you have to do may be to attend classes regularly, pay attention and make good notes, and deal with set homework. Similarly, if you are taking a correspondence course you may feel that it is enough to read and understand the course materials, and return any assignments on time. By doing this minimum amount of work you may well be able to pass the examinations at the end of an introductory course. But what should you do if you want to do more than just pass – to develop your interest, master each subject, and do as well as you can in examinations?

Planning your work and recreation

If you intend to do your best work in tests and examinations you must not mind being criticised by anyone who is not as interested as you are in academic subjects, or who likes to pretend either that success is possible without work or that success in study is unimportant.

If no homework is set, or if you have set work in only one subject, take the opportunity to look through your notes on other subjects or to read, in your textbooks, about the topics you have been studying recently in class. To understand things, and remember them, most people need to make a definite effort. But you will find satisfaction in study comes from (1) increasing your knowledge of a subject, (2) the better understanding of your work as things start to fall into place, (3) the better marks you receive in tests, which encourage you to try to do even better work, and (4) the better grades you achieve in examinations.

You will also find that other people, including teachers and employers, are more inclined to help those who show by their own effort and performance that they are interested in their work and are trying to help themselves.

In planning your own work it is of course up to you to find *ways of working that suit you best*, but to study effectively your work must be *organised*. As in doing set homework (see p. 38), you will probably find that you achieve more if you study two or three subjects in one evening or break up your study of one subject into distinct tasks, devoting about 30 to 50 minutes to each, instead of working for two or three hours at just one task. By exercising self-discipline and keeping to your own plan of work you will derive satisfaction from completing each study task and will then be free to relax and enjoy your recreation.

If you are taking a correspondence course you will receive study materials and set work regularly by post, and it will be up to you to plan when you will do such reading and learning as is necessary, and when you will work on any assignments (e.g. solving problems, preparing written answers, and undertaking practical work). You will have to keep up to date with current work and post completed answers for marking on time, so that (1) you have time to review your progress in each subject, look through your notes and refresh your memory, and (2) you are ready to receive (*a*) the marked assignments returned with comments for your consideration, and (*b*) the next batch of study materials with further assignments.

Concentrating when you work

Where you work: suitable conditions for study
To maintain concentration when you are studying, try to ensure that you have good working conditions:

1 Work in a quiet place where you will not be disturbed by other people talking, listening to the radio, or watching television.
2 Choose a chair that is the right height for you to sit upright and comfortably whilst reading or writing.
3 Have on your working surface just the few books and papers needed for the task you are working on at the time.
4 Ensure that your working surface is sufficiently but not too brightly illuminated, and check that your hand does not cast a shadow on the paper where you are writing.
5 Work in daylight when you can, and with an open window, but do not sit so close to the window that you can see interesting things outside that are likely to attract your attention.
6 Try to work where it is neither so cold that you cannot concentrate nor so hot and stuffy that you feel sleepy.

How you work: your attitude to study
Maintaining attention, whether you are observing, listening, reading or trying to remember, depends on your curiosity or interest. Interest alone does not ensure success, but without interest you are unlikely to maintain your initial resolve to study, throughout each working day and from week to week.

Without interest, in study as in any other employment in which thought is required, you will not do your best work. It is necessary, therefore, either to have or to develop an interest in all aspects of your course.

Developing your interest

1 Where possible, as in practical work and in everyday life, try to observe things for yourself.
2 Try to see connections between new topics and your earlier studies, so that you can associate additions to your knowledge with things you already know and understand.
3 Look for links between the subjects you are studying: your interest in one may be the starting point for developing your interest in another.
4 Use the index of your textbook and consult appropriate reference books so that you can clarify any difficult point quickly and so maintain a firm foundation for further studies.
5 Ask questions if there is any aspect of the work in progress or already completed that you do not understand. Talk about your work with people who share your interests.
6 Look at relevant books and magazines, and at articles in good newspapers, and listen to talks on radio or television which relate your subjects to current affairs.

Making good use of your time

Time management is important in study. As in any work, someone has to decide what needs to be done, when it must be done, and how it is to be completed in the time available. In your studies the course content is set out in the syllabus, in your class notes, and in the recommended textbook. The date of the examination is fixed by the examiners. But only you can decide how to use your time.

Do not postpone your studies until you feel like work. Instead, prepare a realistic timetable or schedule for your work and play, and then do your best to stick to it. This is the way to make sure that you devote enough time to each subject.

Students are sometimes advised to note the times of day when they work best, and to study at these times. For example, most people work best in the morning and early evening. However, in examinations and in any career, you will have to do your best work at times chosen by other people. For example, most examinations are held in the late morning and early afternoon. It is necessary, therefore, to develop your ability to concentrate on any task at any time of day.

So that you can do this, (*a*) do not over-eat, (*b*) devote enough time each day to recreation, including some form of exercise, and (*c*) make sure you have eight hours' sleep each night.

Improving your study skills

Deciding when you will study

Write the days of the week, including Saturday and Sunday, in the left-hand margin of a sheet of wide-lined A4 notepaper. Assuming that you will be in bed from eleven at night until seven in the morning, draw vertical lines to make sixteen columns (one for each of the remaining hours of the day). Then allocate regular times for meals.

If you are attending a full-time course, write in the subjects you study in each organised class. Leave spaces for free periods that could be used for private study or recreation. Then consider how you can best use these periods, and how much time you should devote to study in the evenings and at weekends so that you can complete any set work to your own satisfaction and master each of your subjects as you go along.

If you are employed in some other work during the day, and taking a part-time course, again write in the subjects you study in each organised class and then consider what further study time you need if you are to give a good account of yourself in both course work and examinations. Obviously, because of your other commitments, you are unlikely to be able to take as many subjects as a full-time student. But in the subjects you do study you will be expected to reach the same standard as a full-time student. You will need to keep up with any set work and master each of your subjects.

Similarly, if you enrol for a correspondence course do not take on more work than you could complete satisfactorily in the time available, bearing in mind your other commitments.

As a full-time or part-time student, working a six- to eight-hour day at college or in some employment, you could devote two to three hours to study in the evening, and eight hours to sleep at night, and still have five or six hours to devote to other things (including recreation). This is not to say that you should study *every* evening, but a full-time student might well study on four week-day evenings and a part-time student with organised classes on one or two evenings could devote two other evenings to study.

In preparing for examinations to be taken at the age of 16+, if you are studying full-time, it should be sufficient to work for two hours on each of four evenings, during the week, and for four hours at the weekend (perhaps in two two-hour sessions). But in preparing full-time for examinations to be taken at the age of 18+ you may work for up to three hours on each of four evenings and for up to six hours at the weekend (perhaps in two three-hour sessions).

It is also worth while to set aside a few hours each week that could be used for study if you fall behind in any subject, or if extra work is needed at any time during your course.

Allocating study periods to each of your subjects

Having decided *when* you are going to study, decide which subject you will study in each study session – to ensure that enough time every week is devoted to each of your subjects.

You may find it best to arrange a private study period for a particular subject soon after you have worked at this subject in class (see p. 12). You can then look over class notes, relate new work to previous work, and be ready for the next class on this subject.

Also bear in mind, if you study more than one subject in a single study session, that it is probably best to work at different kinds of subjects. For example, studying one language might interfere with your study of another if you worked on them both on the same evening.

Do not make the mistake of devoting extra time to your best subjects, so that others which really need more attention are neglected. If necessary, allocate extra time to your weakest subjects and to any aspect of your work that you are finding difficult, in an effort to overcome any difficulties that are hindering your progress.

It is probably best to tackle things that you expect to find most difficult in the first hour of a study session, while you are fresh. Then, after studying for about an hour, take a ten-minute break before making a fresh start on another piece of work.

Some people like to save their favourite subjects for the end of a study session. This helps to prevent them spending more time on these subjects than on those that they do not yet find as interesting.

Making a note of things you have to do

You will concentrate best if you can complete a clearly defined piece of work in a limited time (as suggested on p. 37). Working to a timetable or schedule will then mean that you can concentrate on one task and put others on one side, knowing that you will have time for them later.

Therefore, list any things that you must do – including homework and other study tasks you have set yourself. Number them in your order of priority. Then when you come to study a subject you will not need to waste time deciding exactly what needs to be done.

Different kinds of tasks can be included in your timetabled study periods, bearing in mind both your order of priority and the time available. For example, in reflective reading or whilst completing practical exercises you may maintain attention during long periods, but if you have to memorise something it is probably best to do this in several, short study periods.

A two- or three-hour study session need not be devoted to continuous study. Indeed, it is usually easier to maintain concentration if a longer session is divided into shorter periods, as is done at school or college, with up to an hour devoted to one subject or one task and with short breaks of up to ten minutes between study periods.

Avoid distractions during periods you have allocated to private study by completing any urgent tasks, such as making a telephone call or writing a letter, *before* the time you have allocated to study, and then by adopting regular study habits so that other people will know when you will not want to be disturbed.

Adopting an active approach to study

Listening in class can all too easily become passive, with the result that it is difficult to maintain attention. Instead, participate in class by listening, making notes, and asking questions – so that communication is not one-way.

In private study you undertake set tasks (assignments or homework), or you decide what needs to be done. In both, an *active* approach is recommended.

If you spend long periods just sitting, trying to remember class notes or parts of your textbook, you may find that you remember very little. Instead, scan and skim read to find the parts that are of immediate interest. Study these, asking questions as you read (see p. 33) and then make notes or prepare a summary.

When you are reading or preparing a composition, for example, try to pick out things that you do not understand and to recognise gaps in your knowledge. Then try to overcome any difficulties and to find answers to your questions. By concentrating in this way, on things that need your attention, your work will be challenging and interesting, and you will make progress.

In trying to memorise selected points, do not just sit looking at the points underlined in your notes. This would be passive study. Instead, list the points, put the list on one side, try to recall each point, write the list from memory, check your work, and repeat this exercise at intervals until you make no mistakes. This is active study.

Adopting active study techniques will help to keep you thinking as you study:

1 Think as you listen or read.
2 Make carefully selected brief notes.
3 Think about what you have learnt and relate it to previous work.
4 If necessary, add to or amend your class notes.
5 Think again as you express your thoughts in answering questions on each aspect of your work.
6 Avoid fatigue by arranging your studies in sessions that are usually three hours or less.

The most common fault in teaching, in both schools and colleges, is to devote too much time to conveying information but not enough to encouraging students to develop a spirit of enquiry and to helping them to express their thoughts clearly and simply.

And the most common fault in learning is to devote too much time to listening and reading (passively, see Fig. 3.1A). In study, as much time should be devoted to thinking about your work, consolidating, and using your knowledge and understanding to express your thoughts in your own words, as to acquiring information and ideas by listening, observing and reading (see Fig. 3.1B).

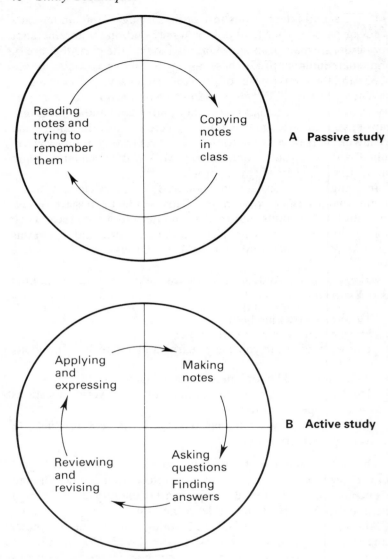

Fig. 3.1 Approaches to study
  A Time allocation in passive study, which is not recommended.
  B Time allocation in active study: making learning a scholarly activity.

Exercises

3.1 Try to plan each piece of work and to organise each study session, and then adopt an active approach to study (as suggested on pp. 37, 39 and 44).

3.2 Try to ensure that wherever you work (see p. 40) you have good conditions for studying.

3.3 Look for ways to develop your interest in each of your subjects (as suggested on p. 41).

3.4 How do you spend your time? Keep a note, for one day, of what you do in each hour. If you think this is a typical day, multiply the times spent on each activity by seven. Are you using your time, each week, in a way that is likely to result in your doing your best in course work and examinations? Are you spending too much, enough, or too little time on each of these activities: (*a*) study (organised classes and private study); (*b*) eating and looking after yourself; (*c*) recreation; and (*d*) sleeping?

3.5 Remind yourself of your reasons for taking your course of study (see Exercise 1.1, p. 14); then prepare a timetable or schedule to show how you plan to spend your time each week until your course is completed (see pp. 42–4).

3.6 Keep an up-to-date list of things you plan to do (as suggested on p. 44) so that, at the start of each private study session, you know exactly what has to be done.

4

Preparing for Tests and Examinations

This chapter encourages you to: (1) keep up to date with course work, (2) review and revise your work as the course develops, (3) ask for help when necessary, and (4) improve your ability to convey your knowledge and understanding in course work, tests and examinations so that you can score higher marks and obtain higher grades.

Will your grades at the end of your course be based solely on your performance in examinations taken at the end, or will your marks for tests and course-work assignments make a contribution?

Find out, at the beginning of your course, when and how you will be assessed. This information, and the syllabuses for each subject you are studying, will be in the regulations of the examining authority responsible for your course. You can consult these in your library, or purchase a copy from the examining authority, or ask each of your teachers how students taking each subject will be assessed.

Keeping up to date with course work

Most of the subjects you study in introductory courses at school, and in vocational courses taken by attendance at a local college or by postal tuition, are examination subjects. You study them not only because they are interesting in themselves, but also because you want to do as well as you can in all assessed work.

If your teachers set regular tests, throughout your course, your best preparation is to listen carefully in class and to read your class notes and homework before each test – because each test will be testing your knowledge and understanding of earlier course work. Look at the notes and diagrams in your notebook to remind yourself of the things your teacher considers important. You are most likely to be asked questions about these things.

Read relevant pages in your textbook, paying particular attention to the things the author emphasises – by sub-headings, numbered lists, and words in **bold** or *italic* print. Consider each point made in the chapter summaries: these should remind you of the most important points – on which you are most likely to be tested.

If your teacher does not set regular homework and class tests, check your own progress as each part of the course is completed by testing yourself. For example, attempt the questions given at the end of the relevant chapter of your textbook.

If you are studying any subject alone, by private study and with no teacher to help, make sure that you buy a textbook that is intended for private study (see p. 18), with questions at the end of each chapter and answers in an appendix or immediately after the questions, so that you can attempt relevant questions and check your own progress.

All your work in the years before an examination increases your knowledge and understanding of your subjects; and getting good marks in tests boosts your self-confidence. The best preparation for examinations that come at the end of your course, therefore, is to work steadily from the beginning (see Fig. 4.1), attend all organised classes, and try to score high marks for all tests and homework.

As you learn and understand more and more about a subject, you put yourself in a position to answer more of the questions set in tests and examinations – so that you can score higher marks if all questions have to be answered and so that you have a better choice. You should again be able to score higher marks, if only some of the questions have to be answered.

The kinds of questions you are asked in tests and in homework should be similar to those you will be set in examinations. Therefore, answering questions in tests and for homework not only gives direction to your work but also provides good practice.

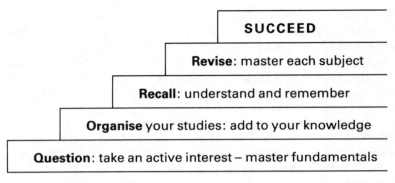

Fig. 4.1   Begin at the beginning: master each subject step by step

Recalling and revising as part of study

Obviously you must complete an aspect of your work before you can revise it, but it is a mistake to complete a whole course and then begin your revision. Study does not come first, occupying the first and major part of the course, with revision in just the last few weeks before examinations: *revision is part of study*.

The work completed in thirty or forty minutes devoted to study, whether this time has been spent in reading or writing, should be followed by recalling what you have achieved and by revision (as recommended on pp. 12 and 33). In perhaps five or ten minutes you can consider what you have been doing and how this fits in with previous work and list the most important points from memory and then check that these are stated correctly.

At the end of each week, plan to devote some time to considering your week's work in each subject and to revision. In this way you can see each week's work in relation to your earlier work, and you can revise new topics while they are fresh in your mind.

Asking for help when necessary

Most teachers look around the class as they speak, to see if anyone is looking puzzled or unsure. They may repeat to make sure that everyone has heard and to give those who did not understand a second chance to consider the words. They may explain things in a different way. Then they may give further explanation or examples, until they feel that each point has been well made.

Teachers usually pause briefly after making an important point, for emphasis and before moving on to the next point. This pause also provides you with the opportunity to make a note and, for example, to ask a question if there is anything that you still do not understand. Relevant questions, during a lesson, might begin:

> Do you mean that . . . ?
> I don't quite understand what you mean by . . .
> What is a . . . ?

And at the end of a lesson most teachers allow time for questions and ask if there are any questions. It is good to ask questions at this time. Suitable questions at this stage might begin with the words:

> If it is true that . . . , how can it be that . . . ?
> Is . . . due to . . . ?
> In . . . , why is there always a . . . ?

A good teacher encourages questions and good students ask questions – which help you and other members of the class to check, clarify and explore.

Questions help teachers to learn what has and what has not been understood, and so help them to improve their teaching. By asking good questions you indicate to a teacher your thoughts about what has been said, and you show interest in the subject.

As far as possible, questions should be asked in class, so that all members of the class can hear the question and benefit from the answer. However, you may also be able to speak to a teacher privately (for example, immediately after a class or during practical work) if you feel that you need more help than can be given in a brief reply to a question asked in class.

If a difficulty arises in your homework or private study, first try to overcome it yourself. Make observations, or refer to your notes, or read your textbook, or consult an appropriate reference book (see p. 24). Then, ask your teacher if you still need help.

Understanding your work as you go along involves overcoming any difficulties as they arise, so that you have a solid foundation upon which to build.

Forming self-help groups

Group discussions are probably most useful for students taking part-time courses, especially adults returning to study some years after leaving school or college, who otherwise would meet people interested in the same subject – and at the same stage in their studies – only once a week.

If the members of a class can meet in twos or threes, perhaps in each other's homes, they can help one another by:

1   keeping current work fresh in the mind;
2   going over class work – learning by confirming that they have understood, by explaining to those who have not yet understood, and by asking and answering questions;
3   discussing current work in relation to earlier studies; and
4   considering the kinds of questions set in tests and other course work, and in examinations, especially as more work is completed and the time for examinations approaches.

In helping one another, any feelings of isolation are avoided. Students reassure one another and make new friends, and each student increases in self-confidence.

Students on full-time courses should also benefit from conversations about their work, between organised classes and in breaks, as well as from discussions organised by their teachers.

And all students can benefit from discussing – in the presence or absence of a teacher – the techniques they use in study. How do you read a book? What do you do between receiving an essay title and handing in the completed essay? How do you respond to corrections, comments, suggestions and marks, written on your work by a teacher? By considering how you work, and how others work, you will find that there is more than one way to tackle most tasks – and you may reconsider and then improve your own study techniques.

Students may benefit not only from considering their teachers' advice and comments written on their own work, but also by looking carefully at work completed by other students who have scored higher marks. Instead of being discouraged by a low mark, try to find out why other students have done better: this analysis is the opposite of considering where you went wrong.

Improving your communication skills

Every teacher, as well as teaching a particular subject, should teach English. Your assessed course work should therefore include not only a mark and notes on any mistakes, misconceptions or misunderstandings concerning the subject of each answer, but also corrections of any mistakes in spelling, punctuation and grammar.

The purpose of each teacher's comments and corrections is first to add to your knowledge and understanding of the subject, and then to help you to prepare effective answers that are a true indication of your ability in this subject.

To score good marks in any subject it is necessary not only to know the answers to the questions asked but also to be able to prepare answers that convey your knowledge and understanding.

In some subjects marks are deducted for mistakes in English, but poor spelling, ineffective punctuation and faults in grammar create barriers between the writer and the reader in any subject in which written answers are required. On the one hand, poor English makes an unfavourable impression and is likely to result, even if indirectly, in the loss of marks. On the other hand, good English makes the reader feel at ease and enables the writer to convey thoughts accurately, clearly, simply and precisely. However you write, therefore, it is worth considering whether or not you could write better. Remember that examiners will know you only by your writing, and that clear writing, like eloquent speech, is the outward sign of clear thinking.

The following statements of the Business and Technician Education Council, in London, indicate the importance examiners attach to good writing:

> 'The ability to speak and write simple English is of major importance in the conduct of affairs at any level. Council believe that the inability to do this effectively is at the root of many problems in business.'

> 'Every teaching programme should aim to develop the student's ability to think, to grasp ideas and to communicate effectively.'

Knowing your words

You need to be sure of the meaning and spelling of every word you use, so that you can use it correctly. In both course work and examinations you must also be sure that you understand every instruction given and every question set. Many students fail to score marks for their answers because they misinterpret the question and so answer the wrong question.

Words are the bricks with which you construct your thoughts. To improve your command of language, (*a*) read articles and books written by people who know how to capture and maintain your interest, and so convey meaning pleasurably; (*b*) take every opportunity to write – especially in course work, when you can benefit from a marker's comments and corrections; and (*c*) consult a textbook or a dictionary whenever you are unsure of either the spelling of a word or its meanings.

Exercise 4.1 Write sentences to make clear the difference in meaning between the following words. Then use a dictionary to check that you have used each word correctly.

accept/except	farther/further
advice/advise	formally/formerly
affect/effect	loose/lose
allowed/aloud	of/off
allusion/illusion	passed/past
beside/besides	practice/practise
board/bored	principal/principle
born/borne	quiet/quite
brake/break	stationary/stationery
canon/cannon	their/there
complement/compliment	to/too/two
dependant/dependent	weather/whether
discreet/discrete	were/where

Meaning

Authors usually explain terms when they first use them. Consult the index of your textbook, therefore, to find the meaning of any unfamiliar term. Also, look at the glossary to see if this includes a concise definition.

The kind of information given in a dictionary is best appreciated by studying entries and making sure you understand all the abbreviations used. These are explained in the preliminary pages of any dictionary, which also include advice on pronunciation and other useful information.

Consider the following examples, which are based on entries in the *Concise Oxford Dictionary*.

Example 1

blōke, n. (colloq.). Man, fellow, chap; the bloke (Nav. sl.), ship's commander. [etym. unkn.]

Explanation
n. = noun
colloq. = colloquial
Nav. sl. = naval slang

Example 2

collō'quial, a. Belonging to familiar speech, not used in formal language (see p. 56).
[f.L. *colloquium*]

Explanation
a. = adjective
f.L. = from Latin

Example 3

slăng, n. Words and phrases used in a special sense by some class or profession, in colloquial use but generally considered in some or all of their uses to be outside standard English.

Explanation
The mark over the ō in *colloquial* indicates that this *o* is pronounced as in 'note'.

The mark over the ă in *slang* indicates that this *a* is pronounced as in 'rack'.

The apostrophe in collo'quial is placed at the end of the stressed syllable.

Such marks are aids to pronunciation.

You may look at a dictionary, therefore, to find the spelling of a word, its origins, its several meanings, an indication of its function (noun, adjective, verb, adverb, etc. – see p. 94), its status in the language (standard English, literal, technical, slang, colloquial, etc.), and examples of its use in appropriate contexts.

Remember, from these examples, that colloquial English and slang belong to spoken English, in appropriate situations, and to reported speech. They may also be used in correspondence between close friends, but are not acceptable in scholarly writing.

In course work and examinations, therefore, write in standard English. Avoid colloquial language, which includes such contractions as *can't* for 'cannot', *isn't* for 'is not', *it's* for 'it is', and *they're* for 'they are'. You are also advised to avoid such meaningless words as *meaningful*, *fabulous*, *fantastic*, *hopefully* and *nice*, which have been devalued by their too frequent use in inappropriate contexts, and to avoid overworked phrases or clichés such as *do your own thing*, *keep a low profile*, *no chance* (meaning not possible), *no way* (meaning not possible), *out of this world*, *over the moon*, and *see the light at the end of the tunnel*.

Spelling

Some people seem to think that correct spelling is unimportant, if the meaning is clear. But unfortunately for those who do not trouble to spell correctly, a mistake in spelling may result in the use of the wrong word. Then the meaning of the sentence may not be clear – although the reader may be able to guess the word that should have been used and the intended meaning of the sentence.

Exercise 4.1 (p. 54) includes some words that are commonly confused. Can you use them correctly?

If your spelling is poor, when you have completed your education, be assured that people who can spell correctly do consider correct spelling to be important and that poor spelling indicates a lack of education. Poor spelling in a letter of application – for a place in higher education or for employment – may result in someone else, not you, being called for interview. Also, poor spelling is a handicap in study and in most professions.

Correct spelling is important. Accept, therefore, if your spelling is not good, that now is the time to make an effort to improve it. The best way to do this is to start a list of words that you find difficult. In this way you can learn from any spelling mistakes corrected in your assessed work. Some words that are frequently mis-spelt are included in Exercise 4.2, but your own list will be better suited to your own needs. Write your list of difficult words again and again, at intervals, with someone reading the words to test you, until you are confident in your spelling.

It is especially important to spell the technical terms of the subject you are studying, and any words used in the question you are answering, correctly.

Exercise 4.2   Ask someone to read these words aloud, as a spelling test, while you write them. Then check your work.

accommodation
achieve
across
advertising
agreeable
almost
apparent
article
beautiful
beforehand
beginning
believe
cannot
changeable
choose
commitment
committee
competence
consensus
definitely
desperate
despite
develop
disappear
dissatisfied

embarrass
equipped
exaggerate
foreign
friend
fulfil
government
guarantee
height
holiday
hopeful
however
independent
interfere
jewellery (*or* jewelry)
leisure
likeable
loser
necessary
ninety
noticeable
occasion
occur *and* occurred
omit *and* omitted
ordinary

parallel
peaceful
peculiar
personnel
preferred
preparation
proceed
procedure
prominent
queueing
relevant
running
secretary
seize
sentence
separate
smiling
sometimes
successful
surprise
tropical
unnatural
until
vicious
unnecessary

Expressing your thoughts clearly
From twenty-six letters the thousands of words of the English language are formed! No two of these words have quite the same meaning and this should make it easy for us to express our thoughts; but each person has a limited vocabulary and each word has more than one meaning. How then is it possible to express thoughts precisely?

Obviously, it helps if you know the several meanings of each of the words you use. Then you can tie the word down in a sentence – with other words – so that the sentence as a whole has only one meaning. It is with a sentence, not usually with an isolated word, that a thought is expressed.

In course work and examinations your readers will not waste their time trying to guess your meaning. And teachers and examiners cannot give marks for what is actually incorrect – even if they think that they know what you probably meant.

Your task as you write is to choose words and arrange them in sentences so that your meaning is clear: you must ensure that you cannot be misunderstood.

Exercise 4.3   What is wrong with each of the following sentences?

1   They only have fish for lunch on Fridays.
2   Since it's inception Britain's longest surviving theatre periodical can also name amongst it's contributors . . .
3   At five years old, my mother took me to my first play.

Answers
1   The meaning is unclear because the word *only* is in the wrong place. Do they have fish on Fridays only, or do they have only fish on Fridays? Do they do anything else, apart from eating fish for lunch, on Fridays?
2   *It's* means *it is*. The possessive pronoun is *its*.
3   Obviously, the child was five – not the mother. To avoid ambiguity, this sentence should read: 'When I was five years old my mother took me to my first play.'

Punctuation
Punctuation marks, used correctly, will help you to ensure clarity and will contribute to the smooth flow of thoughts from your mind to the mind of the reader.

It is possible to write a sentence with no punctuation marks other than the one point that marks the end. The meaning of such sentences may be clear, as in the next paragraph.

Every sentence begins with a capital letter. An exclamation ends with an exclamation mark. A question ends with a question mark. The end of any other sentence is marked by a full stop.

Such writing has its place, for example in examinations when you can say all that is necessary in one sentence or when you are making a list and you wish to complete your answer as quickly and concisely as possible. The use of separate short sentences in a list also makes each item stand out – to attract the examiner's attention – so that you can score marks for every one.

Separate short sentences might also be appropriate in a list of instructions, if you wanted to make sure that each step was simple, clear, and distinct from the next. However, to use only short sentences would be to limit your ability to express your thoughts. Also, instead of aiding communication, short sentences break your writing repeatedly and hinder the reader's progress.

If you have difficulty in putting your thoughts into words, write short sentences and in each sentence express only one thought. But as you gain confidence in using words, closely related thoughts may be linked in one sentence.

Punctuation marks cause the reader to pause for longer than the break between words. This is why they are called punctuation marks or stops. The comma, dash, semi-colon and colon give a progressively longer pause – but they help the writer's thoughts to flow, reducing the number of full stops required, and they help to ensure clarity (to avoid ambiguity).

Note the use of different punctuation marks (comma, dash, semi-colon, full stop, question mark and exclamation mark) in the first four paragraphs of this section (after the heading *Expressing your thoughts clearly*, on p. 57).

Exercise 4.4 Study one paragraph in any composition. Note that each sentence begins with a capital letter and ends with a full stop, question mark or exclamation mark. Consider why each of the other punctuation marks is used.

It pays to know the uses of each punctuation mark so that you can write effective sentences, but use no more than are needed to ensure clarity and easy communication. It also pays to perfect your other sentence writing skills. Because sentences are the units of language in which thoughts are expressed, you are handicapped in any written work unless you can write unambiguous sentences. As with spelling, if you know that you make grammatical errors, now is the time to improve your ability to express your thoughts effectively. The easiest way to do this is to read good prose every day and to write regularly – for example, by preparing notes that are concise but clear and by answering the different kinds of questions set in course work and examinations (see Part Two of this book) so that you have practice in writing throughout your course.

Writing quickly but legibly
For most answers in course work and examinations, marks are given for what you write, not for neat handwriting, but it is important to realise that marks can be given only for words that can be read. Also, in testing a candidate's ability to use language effectively (for example, in an English paper), credit may be given for setting out a composition correctly and effectively, and for neat writing.

In all subjects it is worth making an effort to ensure that your handwriting makes a favourable impression. Improve your writing – if necessary – so that it is quick, confident and easy to read, and so that you can say all that is necessary in the limited time available in examinations.

The writing of children is at first slow, painstaking and uneven, but scholarly writing should be fast, relaxed and flowing. If the pen is raised from the page in forming each letter – as in printing – time is lost (Fig. 4.2A). To write quickly the pen should be held more or

Fig. 4.2 Differences between separate printed letters and a faster, flowing hand.

A   Small (lower case) letters used in printing.
B   More rounded letters, with loops added where necessary so that each letter can be formed in one stroke and joined to the next letter of any word, without raising the pen from the page.
C   Letters of the alphabet joined, as in forming whole words, without raising the pen from the page. These letters are more widely spaced than in written words.

less upright and should feel comfortable. Each letter should be rounded (as in Fig. 4.2B) and so formed that all the letters of each word can be joined in a flowing hand (as in Fig. 4.2C).

Writing is easiest to read if each letter is neither too small nor too large, if words are neither too close together nor too far apart (a space as wide as a letter *w* is about right), and if there are no unnecessary flourishes. Tall letters must stand out above small letters, with *t*'s crossed and *i*'s dotted, and tails must be clearly below the line: wide-lined paper (see p. 13) allows space for such clear writing.

Slow writing is a handicap for a student not only because it limits the number of thoughts that can be conveyed in a given time, but also because the slow writer may have difficulty in maintaining a train of thought.

Black or blue-black inks are best for scholarly writing on white paper. Students are advised not to use other colours, especially red or green, because these are commonly used by teachers and examiners for their comments, corrections and marks.

PART TWO

Question-answering Techniques

In Part Two different kinds of questions which you may be asked in tests and examinations are considered, advice is given on how to tackle them, and exercises are included to give you practice. Similar questions in your course work and in your textbooks will help you to learn about your subjects as well as providing practice. The advice given here, therefore, should help you to score higher marks in course work as well as in tests and examinations.

Your marks in course work, and for the questions set in tests and examinations, will depend not only upon your knowledge and understanding of each of your subjects but also upon your ability to complete effective answers in the time available.

You are therefore advised to consider carefully each question set in course work, before you start preparing your answer, and to look carefully at recent past papers for the tests and examinations that are part of your course so that you can see the kinds of questions you are likely to be asked and consider how best to tackle them.

5

Choosing the Correct Answer

This chapter includes advice on how to tackle the kinds of questions set in so-called objective test papers, including (1) true or false questions, (2) multiple choice questions, (3) multiple response questions, (4) matching pair questions, and (5) assertion–reason questions, in which no writing is required. You score marks by choosing the correct answer or answers from those provided in each question set. Exercises in this chapter comprise questions, with answers, to give you practice.

Objective tests are those in which full marks are given for choosing the correct answer or combination of answers, from those provided, or for indicating if a statement is true or false. But no marks are given for an incorrect answer. Usually all questions must be attempted and the marker or examiner does not have to exercise judgment in deciding whether or not each answer is correct, or in deciding how many marks each answer is worth: both the particular answer required and the marks to be given for this answer are agreed in advance by all those setting the test. This means that all candidates attempt the same questions, and the tests completed by all candidates can be marked in the same way: indeed, many such test papers are marked by computers.

To do well in objective tests it is not enough to remember what has been said in class or what you have read in textbooks. In answering some questions it may be possible to score full marks for things remembered parrot-fashion, even if these are not understood, but most questions test your **understanding**, or your ability to **apply** what you have learned, as well as your **memory**.

You will probably find objective test questions easier than those in which a written answer is required – providing you know your work. You do not have to decide how to answer, as you would if you had to think of the word or words that would best express your thoughts. Also, the statements included in the question – from which you have to select – should jog your memory: you may then recognise the correct answer among the possible answers provided.

Advice on how to tackle different kinds of objective test questions is included in this chapter. For advice on how to tackle test papers, see Chapter 10 (pp. 164–7) which includes an answer to an important question. If you do not know which answer is correct, should you guess?

True or false questions

In a true or false question you have to evaluate a number of statements and judge if each one is true or false. In doing this, always look for qualifying words such as the following, which are here arranged in series:

Quantity
  more, equal, less;
  great, much, little, no;
  all, every, most, many, some, few, none.
Quality
  best, good, bad, worst;
  is, is not; has, has not; does, does not; can, cannot.
Time
  always, invariably, usually, often, sometimes, seldom, never.

To help you decide if a statement is true or false, look for the qualifying word and then try substituting the other qualifying words in the same series to see if any one of them makes the statement more acceptable. Remember that *if a statement is not true in all circumstances, it must be false*.

In true or false questions you can always find a key word or key words upon which the truth or falsity of the statement hinges. Such key words, many of which are qualifying words, are printed in **bold** in each of the statements included in Exercise 5.1.

Exercise 5.1 Decide if each of the following statements is true or false. Make a note of your answers.

(a) Birds **are** the **only** feathered animals.

(b) A red blood corpuscle leaving your lungs **must** pass through your heart **twice** before returning to your lungs.

(c) For photosynthesis green plants **must** have light but they respire at **all** times – day and night.

(d) Mother's milk is a **complete** food for a new-born baby.

(e) Alcohol in small amounts **is** a stimulant.

(f) People who read slowly remember **more** than people who read quickly.

(g) Slow learners have **better** memories than fast learners.

(h) **Logical** thought, starting from **true** premises, **leads** to a **valid** conclusion.

(i) The **smaller** a cube is, the **larger** is its surface area **in proportion to** its volume.

Answers and comments

(a) True. Birds are animals and no other kinds of animals have feathers.

(b) True.

(c) True. Plants like all other living organisms respire at all times but light is essential for photosynthesis.

(d) True.

(e) False. Alcohol depresses the brain even in small amounts.

(f) False, and (g) is also false. Such sweeping generalisations are usually false. There is no doubt that some people who read slowly remember less than some who read quickly; and some fast learners have better memories than some slow learners – and a statement that is not true in all circumstances must be false.

(h) True.

(i) True. Prove this for yourself by calculating the ratio between surface area and volume for small and large cubes.

Multiple choice questions

Multiple choice questions are of two kinds. In one kind, the first few words of the question (called the *stem*) can be combined with each of the endings provided (called *options*) to make a statement that is either true or false. You have to decide which ending is needed to make a true statement. Remember that it is possible to make only *one* true statement: all the others will be false.

In the second kind of multiple choice question, the first part of the question (the stem) may be a question, and you have to decide which of the statements that follow is the correct answer to the question. Once again, only one answer is correct.

In answering a multiple choice question, before choosing the correct ending or the correct answer, you must read the whole question. Do not accept the first statement that seems satisfactory without reading the others carefully. If you do, you may not choose the best of the statements provided. Some statements may be correct as far as they go – yet be incomplete. Others may seem correct at first reading, yet contain mistakes. Remember that all options are so worded as to seem plausible, yet only one is correct.

Therefore, look for the key words, as you would with any true or false statement (see p. 66). Cross out those endings that are obviously incorrect. Then continue to think carefully about the remaining statements, which seem as if they may be true, before deciding which one you think is correct.

Exercise 5.2   Note your answers to the following multiple choice questions. In a test you would probably be asked to underline each ending selected or to mark it in some other way.

1   Which one of the following meanings of the word *principle* is correct?
  - (*a*)   a general law
  - (*b*)   chief
  - (*c*)   original sum invested
  - (*d*)   a stop on an organ
  - (*e*)   parts of verb from which the others can be derived

2 Which ending is needed to make a true statement in each of the following?

  (*a*) The nearest planet to the sun is:
- (i) Pluto
- (ii) Earth
- (iii) Mars
- (iv) Venus
- (v) Mercury

  (*b*) The planet Earth orbits the sun once every:
- (i) 24 hours
- (ii) 7 days
- (iii) 14 days
- (iv) 28 days
- (v) 365 days

  (*c*) The moon orbits Earth once every:
- (i) 7 days
- (ii) 14 days
- (iii) 21 days
- (iv) 28 days
- (v) 365 days

  (*d*) Tides on Earth are caused by the gravitational pull of:
- (i) the moon alone
- (ii) the sun alone
- (iii) the moon and sun
- (iv) the planets
- (v) the sun and stars

3 Arteries differ from veins in that they always carry:
- (*a*) oxygenated blood
- (*b*) blood towards the heart
- (*c*) deoxygenated blood
- (*d*) blood away from the heart

Note that multiple choice questions may be laid out in different ways, and that each question on a test paper may be one multiple choice item (as in questions 1 and 3 here) or it may comprise a number of multiple choice items (as in questions 2, 4 and 5). *Note also* that each item may include four options (as does question 3) or five options (as do questions 1 and 2).

4   Read the following extract from one of Colin Watson's wickedly funny crime novels, *Hopjoy Was Here* (Methuen, London), carefully. Then answer the multiple choice questions which test your comprehension.

The Chief Constable of Flaxborough, Mr Harcourt Chubb, received his London visitors with a degree of affability that he calculated would fall just short of making them feel entitled to put him to any trouble. He
5 introduced Purbright, who found Ross's handshake a shade prolonged and somewhat exploratory, and Pumphrey's over-firm, like that of a man for ever determined to make his first friend.

All but Mr Chubb sat down. He stepped back and
10 relaxed his tall, lean body against the mantelpiece, with one arm extended along it.

Ross glanced at him, then at Purbright.

'I assume, inspector, that Mr Chubb has explained the nature of our interest in this little affair of yours at . . .
15 Flaxborough.' The small hesitation was eloquent of the orientation difficulties of the much travelled. Perhaps the day before it had been Istanbul or Adelaide that needed to be slotted into some similar interview.

Purbright inclined his head. 'I do understand that one
20 of these missing people, a man called Hopjoy, happens to be . . .'

'. . . One of our fellows, yes.' Ross completed the identification with brisk despatch, then looked intently at Purbright. 'Of course, you see how we might be
25 placed?'

'Not precisely, sir.'

   (*a*)   Which one of the following words is closest in meaning to 'affability' as used in line 3?
      A   hostility
      B   interest
      C   indifference
      D   enthusiasm
      E   friendliness

(b)   Who was Purbright (line 5) meeting for the first time?
    A   Chubb
    B   Ross
    C   Chubb, Ross and Pumphrey
    D   Ross and Pumphrey
    E   Chubb and Ross

(c)   Purbright said 'Not precisely, sir' (line 26) because he:
    A   just did not understand
    B   wanted to know more
    C   was trying to be difficult
    D   was being respectful
    E   was being disrespectful

(d)   Do you think Ross hesitated . . . (line 15):
    A   because he was tired?
    B   to capture Purbright's attention?
    C   to give himself time to think?
    D   for effect?
    E   because his mind was wandering?

(e)   All except one of the following statements are true. As far as you can judge from the extract, which one is *untrue*?
    A   The Chief Constable left all explanation to Ross.
    B   Pumphrey had no friends.
    C   Purbright was interested in people.
    D   Ross showed some signs of embarrassment.
    E   Hopjoy was known to the visitors from London.

Note that these multiple choice questions test different **comprehension skills**: (*a*) knowledge of the meaning of a word in a particular context (vocabulary), (*b*) understanding of content (facts), (*c*) understanding of content (implication), (*d*) ability to appreciate more than is actually said (inference), and (*e*) the ability to sum up a situation from the information provided (to summarise).

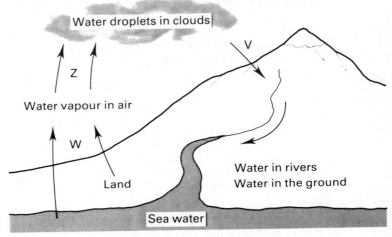

Fig. 5.1   Diagram representing the water cycle

5   In the diagram (Fig. 5.1):
  (*a*)   What does the arrow labelled Z represent?
              A   precipitation
              B   condensation
              C   evaporation
              D   decomposition

  (*b*)   What does the arrow labelled W represent?
              A   transpiration
              B   respiration
              C   condensation
              D   evaporation

Answers to questions in Exercise 5.2
  1 (*a*);   **2***a* (v),   **2***b* (v),   **2***c* (iv),   **2***d* (iii);   **3** (*d*);   **4***a* (E),   **4***b* (D),
  4*c* (B),   **4***d* (D),   **4***e* (B);   **5***a* (B),   **5***b* (D)

As indicated by the examples in this exercise, multiple choice questions can be used to test students of all subjects – and they can be used to assess not only **knowledge** and **understanding** but also the ability to **analyse** or **interpret** information.

Multiple response questions

Each multiple response question, like a multiple choice question, is a set of true or false statements. Again, the first words of the question are a stem which can be combined with each of the endings provided, to make a statement that is either true or false. The difference between this and the multiple choice question is that in a multiple response question *more than one* of the statements is true.

As with a multiple choice question, you must read the whole question before making your answer. Care is needed in selecting statements that are true. The wording of the question will indicate clearly if you have to select one correct statement (multiple choice) or more than one correct statement (multiple response).

Exercise 5.3   A knowledge of first aid is essential for nurses and is useful for anyone. Each of the questions in this exercise is followed by five answers. Note which answers are true and which are false. In a test of this kind you would probably be asked either to tick one of the boxes next to each answer or to mark your answer in a similar way on a separate answer sheet.

		Yes	No
1	Nurses are taught first aid so that they can:		
A	preserve life after an accident	☐	☐
B	practise bandaging	☐	☐
C	prevent further injury after an accident	☐	☐
D	learn biology	☐	☐
E	reassure injured people and promote recovery	☐	☐
2	A patient suffering from cold exhaustion (hypothermia) should be:		
A	kept dry	☐	☐
B	given an alcoholic drink	☐	☐
C	sheltered from the wind	☐	☐
D	warmed slowly	☐	☐
E	warmed quickly	☐	☐

3 Bandages are used:

Yes   No

    A   to keep a dressing in position ☐ ☐
    B   to apply pressure to a wound ☐ ☐
    C   to stop blood flowing into a limb ☐ ☐
    D   to support an injured limb ☐ ☐
    E   to immobilise a broken limb ☐ ☐

4 If bleeding from an injured limb, which is not fractured, is more than minimal:

    A   press a sterile dressing on the wound ☐ ☐
    B   raise the limb ☐ ☐
    C   lower the limb ☐ ☐
    D   apply a tourniquet ☐ ☐
    E   apply pressure to an artery if the bleeding does not stop ☐ ☐

5 To treat a burn:

    A   flush with clean cool water for one minute ☐ ☐
    B   flush with clean cool water for five minutes ☐ ☐
    C   remove any clothing stuck to the burn ☐ ☐
    D   apply an ointment ☐ ☐
    E   apply a sterile dressing ☐ ☐

6 If someone is unconscious:

    A   if necessary start resuscitation ☐ ☐
    B   clear the mouth of any obstruction ☐ ☐
    C   ensure the tongue does not block the throat ☐ ☐
    D   place on side with one leg bent for support ☐ ☐
    E   give a warm drink ☐ ☐

Answers to multiple response question

	1		2		3		4		5		6	
	Yes	No	Yes	No	Yes	No	Yes	No	Yes	No	Yes	No
A	☒	☐	☒	☐	☒	☐	☒	☐	☐	☒	☒	☐
B	☐	☒	☒	☐	☒	☐	☒	☐	☒	☐	☒	☐
C	☐	☒	☒	☐	☐	☒	☐	☒	☐	☒	☒	☐
D	☐	☒	☒	☐	☐	☒	☐	☒	☒	☐	☒	☐
E	☒	☐	☒	☐	☒	☐	☒	☐	☒	☐	☐	☒

Matching pair questions

Some objective test questions include two lists (see questions in Exercise 5.4). You have to match each of the items in one list with the correct item from the other list so as to form a true statement. To answer such a question, proceed as follows.

1 Read both columns quickly.
2 Start with the first item (*a*) at the top of the left-hand column.
3 Compare this with the first item in the right-hand column (A), and then with the second (B), and so on.
4 When you are sure of the best match, write the appropriate letter in the space provided for your answer (e.g. *a*:B in question 1, Exercise 5.4).
5 Continue with the second item in the left-hand column (*b*), and then the third, and so on – matching first the pairs you find easy to put together.
6 As you complete each part of the question, in a test or examination, lightly cross out the entries in both columns – so that you can see clearly what still has to be done.
7 If you are not sure of the best match for any item, go on to the next one.
8 When you have completed the parts of the question you find easy, you will be left with fewer choices to make – to match the remaining items. Note, however, that the second list includes more items than the first, so you cannot work just by a process of elimination.

Exercise 5.4 Note your answers to the following matching pair questions.

1 Which of the cities (A to G) is the capital of each of the countries (*a* to *f*)?

a	Italy	A	Canberra
b	Bulgaria	B	Rome
c	Brazil	C	Sofia
d	United States of America	D	Bucharest
e	Rumania	E	Brazilia
f	Australia	F	Washington
		G	Budapest

2 Which of the definitions (A to G) is correct for each of the terms (*a* to *f*)?

a	verb	A	word used to describe or qualify a noun or pronoun
b	pronoun		
c	adjective	B	word that governs and marks the relation between a noun or pronoun and some other word in a sentence
d	adverb		
e	preposition		
f	conjunction		
		C	a word that indicates action
		D	word used instead of a noun so that the noun need not be repeated
		E	word that is the name of a thing
		F	word used to join parts of a sentence or to make two sentences into one
		G	word that modifies a verb, an adjective or an adverb

3 Which of the discoveries in list 1 was made by each of the scientists in list 2?

	Discovery		*Scientist*
a	vaccination against smallpox	A	Jenner in 1789
b	bacteria can cause disease	B	Semmelweis in 1846
c	fungus *Penicillium* prevented growth of bacteria in culture dish	C	Pasteur in 1866
d	hand-washing helps to prevent spread of disease	D	Lister in 1876
e	antiseptic surgery		

4 Which of the plane figures (*a* to *e*) in list 1 has the number of sides and angles stated next to each item (A to F) in list 2?

	List 1		*List 2*
a	pentagon	A	10
b	square	B	5
c	hexagon	C	3
d	octagon	D	6
e	decagon	E	4
		F	8

5 Which of the symbols (A to F) in Fig. 5.2 represents each of the electrical/electronic components (*a* to *e*) listed next to the figure?

Components

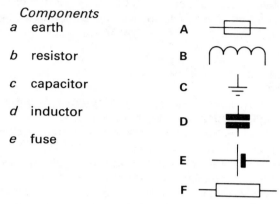

a earth	A
b resistor	B
c capacitor	C
d inductor	D
e fuse	E
	F

Fig. 5.2 International Electrotechnical Commission recommended graphical symbols for electrical power and electronic diagrams

Answers to matching pair questions

	1	2	3	4	5
a	B	C	A	B	C
b	C	D	C	E	F
c	E	A		D	D
d	F	G	B	F	B
e	D	B	D	A	A
f	A	F			

Note that each matching pair question is a kind of completion test (see p. 93), in which you are given the words needed to complete a true statement. For example, in question 1, Canberra (A) is the capital city of Australia (*f*). And in question 2, a verb (*a*) is a word that indicates action (C). Words from the question, with words from the two lists, are used to make true statements.

Assertion–reason questions

Some questions comprise two statements. You have to consider each of these statements and decide whether they are true or false. And if both are true you have to decide whether or not the second is the correct explanation of the first. To answer such questions, proceed as follows.

1   Read the first statement (*a*) carefully and decide whether or not it is correct.
2   Delete the word true or false, as appropriate, if spaces are provided next to the first part of each answer.
3   Read the second statement (*b*) carefully and decide whether or not it is correct.
4   Delete the word true or false, as appropriate, if spaces are provided next to the second part of each answer.
5   If both statements (*a* and *b*) are true, decide whether or not the second is the correct explanation of the first.
6   Record your answer according to the instructions on your test paper.

Exercise 5.5   Record your answers to each of the following assertion–reason questions, as follows.

Record

    A   if *a* and *b* are true
        and *b* is the correct explanation of *a*,
or **B**   if *a* and *b* are true
        but *b* is not the correct explanation of *a*,
or **C**   if *a* is false but *b* is a true statement.
or **D**   if *a* is true but *b* is a false statement.

1   (*a*)   Green plants excrete oxygen on warm sunny days.
    (*b*)   In green plants in daylight, photosynthesis usually proceeds more rapidly than respiration.

2   (*a*)   It is best to photograph scenery on clear sunny days.
    (*b*)   The smaller the aperture of a camera, the greater the depth of field.

3   (*a*)   On-shore breezes are strongest on hot days.
    (*b*)   On hot days the sea warms up quicker than the land.

4 (a) Wet clothes, hung out to dry in the open air, dry fastest in hot calm weather.

(b) Warm air can hold more water vapour than cooler air.

5 (a) Perspiration does not help to keep the body cool in hot weather if the air is already saturated with water vapour.

(b) Heat energy in the environment can be absorbed in the change of state from liquid water to water vapour only if the air is not already saturated with water vapour.

6 (a) The longest day in the northern hemisphere is on 21st June, and in the southern hemisphere this is the shortest day.

(b) The tropic of cancer is nearest to the sun on 21st June; therefore the tropic of capricorn is furthest away at this time.

7 (a) We see colours by sunlight but not by moonlight.

(b) Our eyes contain two types of light sensitive cells: one kind, called cones, are colour sensitive but they do not function at low light intensities.

8 (a) White clothes are best if you want to keep cool in hot weather and warm in cold weather.

(b) White clothes absorb more heat than do coloured clothes.

9 (a) Shakespeare wrote 'Shall I compare thee to a summer's day'.

(b) When in a literary work one thing is compared with another, such a figure of speech is called a simile.

10 (a) In temperate climates, some plants that flower in spring sometimes flower again in the autumn.

(b) Flowering in most plants is a response to day length.

Answers to assertion–reason questions

1 A, **2** B, **3** D, **4** C, **5** A, **6** A, **7** A, **8** D, **9** B, **10** A

Exercise 5.6 You should recognise the following questions as multiple choice, multiple response, and assertion–reason questions, even though the layout of each question and the choices provided differ from those in the questions in Exercises 5.2, 5.3 and 5.5.

1 If the sales of a firm are $24 000, the cost of sales $12 000 and expenses $4000, the net profit is:

    A $4000
    B $8000
    C $12 000
    D $20 000

2 Which of the following is/are usually subject to depreciation?

    (1) Plant and machinery
    (2) Motor vehicles
    (3) Freehold land

Answer this question using the following code:
answer: **A** if 1, 2 and 3 are correct
        B if 1 and 2 are correct
        C if only 1 is correct
        D if only 3 is correct
        E if none of the options are correct

3 To answer this question, decide if the assertion, reason and argument are as indicated next to the letter A, B, C, D or E.

	ASSERTION	REASON	ARGUMENT
A	True	True	Reason a correct explanation
B	True	True	Reason not a correct explanation
C	True	False	Not applicable
D	False	True	Not applicable
E	False	False	Not applicable

ASSERTION		REASON
A variety chain store is a combination of a Department store and a Multiple shop	*because*	it is mainly sited in town and city centres.

Answers: **1** B, **2** B, **3** B

6

Giving Short Written Answers

This chapter includes advice on how to tackle the kinds of questions that require short written answers: one word, one phrase, one sentence, or one paragraph. Questions with specimen answers are included, plus exercises to help you improve your writing and to practise answering questions of this type.

As with other types of questions, most short-answer questions test not only that you have remembered what you have been taught or what you have read, but also that you have understood. This is why learning by heart – so-called rote learning – is usually a waste of time as a method of preparing for tests and examinations.

Some questions are in parts, testing *first* that you can **remember** certain facts, rules, laws, etc.; *second* that you **understand** them; and *third* that you can (*a*) **apply** your knowledge and understanding in solving a problem, or (*b*) **analyse** information provided in the question or remembered from course work, or (*c*) bring together information from different sources (**synthesise**) and reach some conclusion or express some opinion, or (*d*) **evaluate** the strengths and weaknesses of an argument or the evidence for or against a point of view.

In short written answers you must give all the information asked for in the question, but remember that a satisfactory answer – for which you can score full marks – may be given in one short paragraph, in a concise sentence or phrase, or even in one word. Therefore, keep each of your answers short and to the point.

You may know how many marks are available for a question. This may be stated next to the question (as on p. 83), or all questions on the paper may be allocated equal marks (e.g. fifty questions with a maximum of two marks available for each answer). The number of marks available for each answer is an indication of the length of the answer expected by the examiners (see p. 84). And if your answers have to be written immediately after each question, on an answer sheet, or in an answer book, the amount of space left for your answer (see pp. 97–8) also indicates the maximum length of the answer expected by the examiner.

To help you score full marks for each question you answer, remember that your teacher or examiner will be looking for a particular point (or for a limited number of main points, see p. 20) in each of your answers. This list of points is the examiners' *marking scheme*. If you include one of these points in your answer you will usually be given credit for it; but try to include only relevant material, so that you will score a mark (or marks) for every point that you make.

The purpose of the marking scheme, which is used by all examiners marking a particular set of examination papers, is to try to ensure that all papers are marked in the same way – so that all candidates are treated fairly. Note that this method of marking is different from the marking of an objective test, in which your answer is bound to be either right or wrong (see p. 65). Your knowledge and understanding, as displayed in your written answers, may not be entirely correct – or altogether incorrect. Tests and examinations in which written answers are required (as in the kinds of questions considered in this chapter and in Chapters 7 and 8) are therefore said to be *subjective*: the examiner has to exercise judgment in deciding how many marks each answer is worth.

The shorter or more concise a written answer has to be, the more it becomes an objective rather than a subjective test of your knowledge and understanding. Indeed, some short-answer questions are so worded that a definite answer is required (such as *oxygen*, *blue*, *first*, and *yes*). As in true or false questions (Chapter 5), only one answer can be accepted as correct. Such questions are called *closed questions* (see also pp. 116–22). In contrast, other questions are said to be *open ended* (see pp. 122–5) because the writer has more freedom in deciding what should be included.

Answering with one or two words

In a two- or three-hour examination in which you have to answer only four or five questions, you will probably be expected to divide your time equally between the questions. Therefore, if a question began with the words:

> Do you consider that . . .

it would be a mistake to answer simply 'Yes' or 'No'. But to ensure that no candidates give such short answers, when more is required, examiners are unlikely to start questions in this way. Instead, they ask you to:

> Explain why some people consider that . . .
> *or* Summarise the arguments for and against the view . . .

Similarly, in a test in which you had to answer many questions, each question should be so worded as to make clear the length of answer required. But if you are not sure how much to write, remember that the amount of space available for your answer, and the number of marks available, also provide a guide. Many students waste time that could be spent on other questions, and indicate that they are not sure what the examiner wants to know, by writing far more than is necessary for a complete and correct answer.

Exercise 6.1   Each of the following questions, which could be set in a first examination in science, requires only one or two words either to answer the question, or to answer each part of the question.

1   Name the seven essential constituents of a balanced diet for people.

....
....
....
....

(14 marks)

2   In the circulation of blood, how many times does a red blood corpuscle pass through your heart between leaving the pulmonary artery and returning to this vessel?

....

(2 marks)

3   Name one constituent element of all oxide molecules.

....

(2 marks)

4   Name two substances, in addition to iron, that must be present before iron will rust.

....

(4 marks)

5   Fresh water is less dense than sea water. Is the pressure 25 m below the surface of the sea less, the same, or greater, than the pressure 25 m below the surface of fresh water?

....

(4 marks)

6   Fresh air is a mixture of gases. Which of these gases:

(*a*)   forms about four-fifths of the atmosphere,

....

(*b*)   may comprise up to seven per cent of a sample of fresh air or be absent from the sample,

....

(*c*)   is essential to life but may be used only by certain bacteria (not by animals or plants),

....

(*d*)   is produced by green plants during photosynthesis,

....

(*e*)   is produced in the aerobic respiration of green plants,

....

(*f*)   is absorbed from the air and used by green plants in photosynthesis,

....

(*g*)   is used at all times by living organisms that cannot respire anaerobically,

....

(*h*)   condenses to form clouds and mists?

....

(16 marks)

Answer to questions in Exercise 6.1

1	carbohydrates	vitamins
	proteins	mineral salts
	lipids	roughage
		water

2	Twice	
3	Oxygen	
4	Water	Oxygen
5	Greater	
6	*a*	Nitrogen
	b	Water vapour
	c	Nitrogen
	d	Oxygen
	e	Carbon dioxide
	f	Carbon dioxide
	g	Oxygen
	h	Water vapour

Answering with a phrase

Some short-answer questions can be answered in a few words: a complete sentence is not necessary. Once again, the less time you spend in writing the more you can spend in thinking – or in answering other questions.

Exercise 6.2   Each of the following general knowledge questions requires either a phrase to answer the question or a phrase to answer each part of the question.

1   How many hours' sleep are required each night by anyone aged sixteen to twenty-one years?

....

2   What causes ocean currents?

....

3   State four functions of money.

....
....
....
....

4   State four factors which an employer must consider before deciding on the location of a new factory.

....

....

....

....

5   State three reasons for the movement of people from rural to urban areas which is occurring in many so-called under-developed countries.

....

....

....

Answers to questions in Exercise 6.2

1   Eight to nine hours
2   The prevailing winds
3   A medium of exchange
   A unit of account
   A store of value
   A standard of deferred payment
4   The availability of suitable labour
   The costs of transporting raw materials
   The costs of distributing products to their markets
   The availability and cost of suitable premises
5   Deterioration of farm land
   The hope of finding paid employment in towns
   The desire for a more comfortable lifestyle

Answering with one sentence

A sentence differs from a phrase in that it makes sense by itself, even if you do not know the context in which it fits. Whereas a phrase may be used in answer to some questions (as in questions 1 and 2 in Exercise 6.2), or in obeying an instruction (as in questions 3, 4 and 5 in Exercise 6.2), at least a sentence is necessary if anything is to be defined, described or explained.

Exercise 6.3 Each of the following questions on economics and economic geography can be answered in the space provided, in one sentence. Obviously, more detailed answers would also be possible, and would be desirable if the time allowed in an examination or if the space allowed in an examination or test answer book indicated that longer answers were required.

1 What geographic factors should influence an employer's choice of a location for a new factory?

....
....
....

2 In a nation's economy why is a deficit on current account a greater cause for concern than a deficit on the balance of trade?

....
....
....

3 What is invisible trade?

....
....
....

4 Define birth rate.

....
....

Answers to questions in Exercise 6.3

1 The geographic factors an employer should consider are the availability of suitable labour, power and water supplies; the availability of raw materials; access to markets; and transport facilities.

2 A deficit on current account is of greater concern because it includes payments for all goods and services, whereas a deficit on the balance of trade in goods may be offset by payments for services.

3 Invisible trade is the movement of money in or out of a country for services (e.g. transport charges, banking and insurance charges, interest on investments, and receipts for tourism).

4 Birth rate is the number of live births per year per thousand of the total population.

Note that the answers to questions 3 and 4 are definitions. To prepare a good definition it is necessary to know the rules. First state the general class to which the thing you are defining belongs, and then state how the particular thing you are defining can be recognised. A definition must apply to all things known by the term you are defining, but it must apply to nothing else. It should be as simple and concise as possible. Most definitions are written in one sentence.

It is sometimes useful, after a definition, to give an example – and this is usually desirable in tests and examinations even if an example was not asked for in the question – but the example is not part of the definition.

Answering in one paragraph

One paragraph, a number of sentences devoted to a single topic, may be a complete answer to a question: a concise composition. The first sentence of a paragraph is usually what is called the *topic sentence*: it tells the reader what the paragraph is to be about.

When you are writing only one paragraph, the topic sentence will probably give the essence of your answer. The sentences that follow will then give supporting information and perhaps an example.

Any sentence should convey one idea or a few closely related ideas; and the sentences in a paragraph should, if possible, be arranged in an appropriate order. In some paragraphs, if you are presenting evidence, your topic sentence may come at the end. It is then your conclusion: your most important point.

Exercise 6.4   Study the sentences in any composition. Note that they are arranged in paragraphs. Each paragraph deals with one topic, and one sentence (usually the first) indicates what this topic is.

Study one paragraph. Pick out the topic sentence and note how the other sentences are related to it. Note that the sentences vary in length but that each one, by itself, makes complete sense. It expresses either one thought or a few closely related thoughts. The last sentence either ties the whole paragraph together or helps, if further paragraphs follow, to make connections.

For example, study the following paragraphs. The first is from *Private Angelo* by Eric Linklater, the second from *The Deceivers* by John Masters, and the third from *For Kicks* by Dick Francis.

1   In the morning the face in his shaving mirror looked at him so whitely, from such dark enormous eyes, that he was at first startled and then impressed by it. His cup of warm water grew cold while he studied it. It was the reflexion, he thought, of a tragic but romantic figure. It was the face, he told himself, of a man of destiny. It had caught its pallor from the coldness of fate, and he could not avoid his allotted task however deeply his eyes might mourn the necessity. This perception did not exactly give him courage, but lent him a kind of resignation, or hypnotized his wilder fears, and let him pass the next few days without drawing much attention to his utter unsuitability for service with Force 69.

2   William watched the approaching ferrymen, and his heart sank. As they shuffled forward they looked about them at the soldiers and prisoners. William saw that their faces were closing visibly, like oysters, and veils were coming down across their eyes. Before, when he had talked to them, they had done their best to help him by remembering what they could. They had given him descriptions. Now the men they had described were confronting them. Perhaps they had never expected that. Perhaps they had invented the descriptions in the first place, to satisfy him and get rid of him. Now it was different. These prisoners had not done them, personally, any harm. The court-house was a long way off; cases took a long time to reach the magistrate; who would work the ferry? They had written nothing down on paper. The spoken word could be forgotten, disavowed. It was an inborn habit of India's poor, bred over turbulent centuries of intrigue when the shifts of power made it safer to forget than to remember.

3   His name, I saw from the race card, was Superman. He was not one of the eleven horses I had been investigating: but his hotted up appearance and frantic behaviour, coupled with the fact that he had met trouble at Stafford in a selling chase, convinced me that he was the twelfth of the series. The twelfth; and he had come unstuck. There was, as Beckett had said, no mistaking the effect of whatever had pepped him up. I had never before seen a horse in such a state, which seemed to me much worse than the descriptions of 'excited winners', I had read in the press cuttings: and I came to the conclusion that Superman was either suffering from an overdose, or had reacted excessively to whatever the others had been given.

Note that successive sentences in the first paragraph develop the thought expressed in the first, the topic sentence, and seem to lead inevitably to the last sentence.

The second paragraph is also about what can be seen in the faces of men. Each sentence leads the reader on, adding a thought. The topic sentence comes at the end. The ferrymen will find it safer to forget than to remember.

The third paragraph starts with the topic sentence. The paragraph is about a race horse. Each sentence tells the reader more about this horse and leads to the writer's conclusion – in the last sentence.

Note, in each of these extracts, not only that each sentence is relevant to the topic sentence, but also that you could not delete one word without losing something of the author's meaning or detracting from the effects created in your mind.

Learn from this, and in writing use words to convey your meaning or to create an impression. Make sure that each sentence is relevant to the topic sentence. If it is not, should you have started a new paragraph?

Never introduce words just for padding. Unnecessary words are obstacles to the reader's progress. They make it harder for your teachers or examiners to find the useful words with which you hope to score marks.

Exercise 6.5   Many of the questions set in examinations can be answered in one paragraph. Sometimes the length of answer required is indicated by the space allowed in an answer book, or by the number of marks available (perhaps four or five for such a short answer in a three-hour examination), or by the words of the question (such as 'Explain briefly . . .' or 'Write one paragraph about . . .').

It is worth planning your answer, to make sure that you score the four or five marks available. Make a note of four or five relevant points to be included in your answer, so that the examiner will see in each sentence of your answer a point that is included in the marking scheme and for which a mark is to be given.

Here are some questions that could be set in different subjects. You will probably see similar questions about the subjects you are studying, in the test questions in your textbooks and in your examination papers.

1 Explain why active volcanoes occur only in certain parts of the world.
2 Explain what is meant by a balanced diet for people.
3 Why is it that during a period of inflation some people may benefit financially and others may suffer financially?

Specimen answers to questions in Exercise 6.5

1 Active volcanoes are in parts of the world affected by the last world-wide period of folded-mountain formation; which are associated with faults in Earth's crust. Molten magma, below the hard crust, approaches the surface along deep-seated rifts in the crust – and in certain places erupts from time to time as an active volcano.

2 A balanced diet is one that contains enough of all essential nutrients (carbohydrates, fats and oils, proteins, mineral salts, vitamins), enough roughage, and enough water, needed for healthy living. An imbalance in the diet, due to a deficiency of any one essential – or even to an excess of some essentials – will adversely affect health: that is to say it will cause disease.

3 During a period of price inflation people who obtain regular wage increases that keep ahead of price increases for goods and services may benefit financially – even if only in the short term. On the other hand, people who receive no increase in income (for example, bondholders) will suffer financially; and so will those who obtain regular wage increases that fail to keep ahead of price increases. Even those whose wage increases do keep ahead of price increases may suffer financially – on balance – if they also have investments that provide a fixed income or earn interest at a rate that is below the rate of price inflation.

7

Answering Questions based on Information Provided

This chapter will help you to answer those questions in which information is provided to remind you of the answer, or so that you can work out the answer. Questions with specimen answers are included, plus exercises to help you practise answering questions of this type.

To answer questions based on information provided, you are normally expected to do more than copy selected words from the question into your answer book. The information provided serves as a stimulus which calls for a response, and these are therefore sometimes called *stimulus–response questions*. They test your ability to (1) understand the question, (2) remember course work, and (3) use the information provided in the question *either* by itself *or* supported by your knowledge and understanding of the subject derived from course work.

Calculating the answer

The answers to some questions in which information is provided must be obtained by calculation. Introductory textbooks on subjects in which calculations are required include information and instruction, advice, and questions with specimen answers. If you are studying such subjects you must understand each question and be able to decide how to work out the answer. In addition you must know how to set out each step in your calculation so that a teacher or examiner can see, from your working, how you obtained the answer. Then, even if the answer is incorrect, it is possible to see if the method you adopted was appropriate and where you went wrong. Credit can then be given for the knowledge and understanding displayed.

Answering completion questions

In a completion or fill-in test you are asked to write a word (or a phrase) in each of the spaces left in a sentence or paragraph. If you know your work, the words in each sentence should be enough to indicate which words are missing, so that you can fill each space correctly.

A completion test may be a kind of multiple choice test, in which you are asked to select the correct word or phrase from a list provided (as in questions 2 and 3 on p. 69). Alternatively, you may have to provide the missing word or phrase from memory (as in the questions in Exercise 7.1, below).

You can expect to score one or two marks for each space you fill by inserting the correct word or words. These are the words your examiners expect – which are in their marking scheme (see p. 82). Think carefully, therefore, before you write. The most appropriate word may not be the first word that comes to your mind. Draw upon your knowledge of the subject: select the most appropriate word or phrase.

If you are not sure of the answer – the word needed to fill any space – make a mark in the margin to remind you to reconsider this question later. Then the correct insertion may come to mind; but if you are still not certain perhaps you should make a considered guess. See page 166 for advice on guessing.

Exercise 7.1 Note your answers to the following completion questions. In a test you would probably be asked to insert the missing words in spaces provided as part of the question in your answer book.

1 Air is a mixture of ....A........ . One of these, called ....B........ , comprises about three-quarters of the air by volume, and another, ...C........ , about one-quarter.

2   The difference between a country's visible exports and visible imports is known as the balance of ......D....... .

3   Words are classified according to the work they do in a sentence, and called the parts of speech. Nouns are all ......E........ , and words such as he, she and it that can be used instead of nouns are called ......F...... . ...G..... indicate action. ......H...... describe or qualify nouns or pronouns; and adverbs modify ......I......, ...J....... or other ......K...... . Words such as *and, either* and *or* are called ......L....... because they are used to join the parts of a sentence or to make two sentences into one.

4   A preposition governs and marks the relation between a noun or pronoun and some other word in the sentence, for example:

the relation ..M..	based ......N......
compared ...O...	instead ......P.....
intended ....Q....	better ......R........
different ....S....	preferable......T........

Answers to completion questions in Exercise 7.1

1   A = gases; B = nitrogen; C = oxygen

2   D = trade. Balance of trade is correct, not balance of payments, because balance of payments also includes invisible imports and exports which are excluded from this question by the word visible.

3   E = names; F = pronouns; G = verbs; H = adjectives; I = verbs; J = adjectives; K = adverbs; L = conjunctions.

4   M = between; N = on *or* upon; O = with *or* to; P = of; Q = for; R = than; S = from; T = to. 'Different than' and 'preferable than', used in American English, are unacceptable in British English.

Labelling diagrams

In some questions, instead of sentences with words missing, you may be asked to name parts indicated in a diagram. This is a kind of completion test. The things to be labelled are indicated by labelling lines and usually by a letter, or just by a letter (see Figs 7.1 and 7.2). You are asked to name some or all of the things labelled by letters in the diagram, either by selecting words from a list provided (in a kind of matching pairs test, see Question 5 on page 77) or entirely from memory (as on pp. 95 and 96).

Exercise 7.2

Study Fig. 7.1, then:
1 Name the blood vessels: A ....
  B ....
  C ....
2 State one way in which the blood in vessel A differs from that in vessel X.

....

3 State one way in which the blood in vessel B differs from that in vessel Y.

....

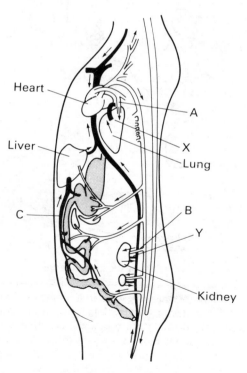

Fig. 7.1 Some parts of the body

Exercise 7.3

Study Fig. 7.2, then:

1   Name the ocean A.
2   Name the seas B and C.
3   Name the rivers D, E, F and G.
4   Name the countries X, Y and Z.

Fig. 7.2   Part of Western Europe

Answering the stimulus–response questions in Exercises 7.2 and 7.3
Exercise 7.2   (1) A = pulmonary artery; B = renal artery; and C = hepatic portal vein. (2) The blood in A differs from that in X in that it contains more carbon dioxide. (3) The blood in B differs from that in Y in that it contains more oxygen. Note that in questions 2 and 3 only *one* difference is required.
Exercise 7.3   Refer to a map of Western Europe in your atlas for the one-word answers to these questions.

Answering case study questions

Case study questions are based on information provided in the form of diagrams or tables, or in writing. Some questions can be answered just by interpreting this information correctly; but for a complete and correct answer to other questions prior knowledge of the subject – from your course of study – is also necessary.

Exercise 7.4

Look at the population statistics in Table 7.1 and at the histograms in Fig. 7.3, based on estimates from the United Nations *Demographic Yearbook 1982*, and then answer the following questions.

Table 7.1 Total population and live births in 1982, for Italy and the Philippines

	Total population	*Live births*
Italy	57 069 701	662 990
Philippines	48 098 460	1 791 328

1 Fewer people live in the Philippines than in Italy.

(*a*) In which age-groups are there more people in the Philippines than in Italy?

....

(*b*) Suggest two reasons why there are more people in these age groups in the Philippines than in Italy.

(i) ....

....

(ii) ....

....

2 (*a*) In which of these two countries will population increase rapidly if present trends continue?

....

(*b*) Suggest two kinds of measures a government might introduce in response to such a prediction of a rapid increase in population.

(i) ....

....

(ii) ....

....

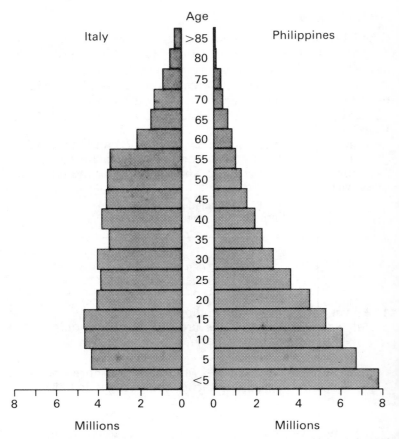

Fig. 7.3   Age structure of the population of Italy and the Philippines in 1982

3   What was the birth rate in Italy and in the Philippines in 1982?
   (*a*)   Italy = ...   (*b*)   Philippines = ...

4   In this age of disease control, automation, robotics, and unemployment of manual labourers, suggest two ways in which young people in an industrial country might be expected to benefit from a decline in the birth rate.
   (i) ....
   (ii) ....

Exercise 7.5

Read this passage, which is based on Burningham, D. Ed. (1984) *Economics* (Sevenoaks, Hodder & Stoughton), and then answer the questions on p. 101.

Market forces left to themselves tend to produce a market-clearing price or equilibrium price (P_e in Fig. 7.4) at which, as a result of the interaction of buyers and sellers, supply equals demand.

On the one hand, if an association of producers tries to fix a minimum price (P_1 in Fig. 7.4) at which supply exceeds demand (by $Q_1 Q_2$, see Fig. 7.4), the surplus will put a downward pressure on price. Distributors will cut prices to clear stocks, and will reduce orders to manufacturers – who in turn will lower their output. Then, as lower prices stimulate demand, the excess of supply will be reduced until the market clearing price is reached. Unless something is done about unsold stocks, therefore, the price-fixers will be defeated in their attempt to establish a minimum price higher than the market-clearing price.

On the other hand, attempts to fix a maximum price (P_2 in Fig. 7.4) below the market-clearing price will tend to produce shortages and so put an upward pressure on price. Rent

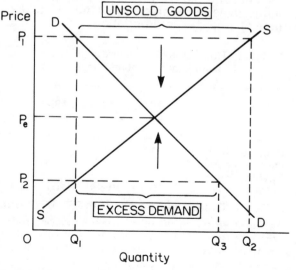

Fig. 7.4   Price fixing. S = supply; D = demand. From Burningham (1984)

controls in the United Kingdom housing market demonstrate the effects of Governments' trying to fix maximum prices – for the hire of living accommodation – below the market level. Rent Acts, restricting the amount of rent a landlord can charge, were first introduced in 1915 to protect tenants from the hardship of high rents caused by what was thought to be a temporary housing shortage. Rent controls have remained, and under the Rent Act of 1977 and the Housing Act of 1980 tenants may apply to a Rent Tribunal for a 'reasonable rent' to be decided.

The long-term effect of these Acts of Parliament has been to create an artificial housing shortage. Because the controlled rents (P_2 in Fig. 7.4) are generally below the market-clearing price, there is an excess of demand over supply (Q_1Q_3 in Fig. 7.4). At this lower price, both the quality and quantity of rentable accommodation is reduced, because the financial incentive to private developers to build new houses and flats solely for renting is weakened, and fixed rents make it impossible for landlords to keep property in good condition. The shortage has been exacerbated because many home owners who might otherwise have let flats or rooms are unwilling to do so as a result of the Rent Acts.

The decline in privately rented dwellings (Table 7.2) has been due in part to the increased demand for home ownership and in part to rent controls. The increased proportion of public sector dwellings gives some indication of the cost to taxpayers of the shortage of rented accommodation.

Table 7.2   Housing stock by tenure in the United Kingdom: millions of dwellings

	1914	1951	1978
Others	—	1.1	1.0
Public sector	0.1	2.5	6.6
Owner occupied	0.9	4.1	11.1
Private rented	7.5	6.2	1.9
Total	8.5	13.9	20.6

To summarise: fixing a minimum price *above* or a maximum price *below* the market-clearing price will not work. It will be necessary to take further steps in attempts to deal with the problems created by the consequent excess of supply or demand.

Now answer these questions:

1 Between 1914 and 1978, in the United Kingdom, by how many has (*a*) the stock of privately rented dwellings declined, and (*b*) the stock of public sector dwellings increased?

2 What percentage of dwellings in the United Kingdom were privately rented in (*a*) 1914, and (*b*) 1978?

3 What percentage of dwellings in the United Kingdom were rented by the public sector in (*a*) 1914, and (*b*) 1978?

4 Do the arguments presented in the passage (pp. 99–100) lead you to conclude that the repeal of the Rent Acts would
   (*a*) increase or decrease the supply of privately rented accommodation; and
   (*b*) increase or decrease the rents charged by private landlords?

5 Explain why guaranteed minimum prices for farm produce, above the free-market price, to encourage investment in agriculture, could lead to excessive stocks of some commodities.

6 What would be the likely consequences of a Government's fixing a maximum price, below the prevailing market price, for a commodity – in an attempt to protect consumers?

Answering the case study questions in Exercises 7.4 and 7.5

Exercise 7.4 The answer to Q1(*a*) can be obtained from Fig. 7.3, and two reasons suggested in answer to Q1(*b*) are (i) the large number of children born in the Philippines (Table 7.1), and (ii) availability of medical treatments and food to allow most of them to survive. Q2(*a*) requires a one-word answer (Philippines), and 2(*b*) can be answered in two phrases: (i) measures to increase the productivity of agriculture; and (ii) measures to encourage a reduction in the birth rate. The answer to Q3 can be calculated from the estimates in Table 7.1 if you know the meaning of the term *birth rate* (see p. 87). Q4 Young people *might be expected to benefit* (i) from the reduced competition for employment during their working lives, and (ii) from a longer working life.

Exercise 7.5 Q1, 2 and 3 can be answered from the estimates in Table 7.2; and Q4, 5 and 6 from Fig. 7.4 plus the explanation given.

Answering questions that require a summary or précis

In some questions you are given a short composition and asked to reduce its length. Such précis writing, which is sometimes called summarising, tests your ability to (*a*) read carefully, (*b*) understand, (*c*) select what is needed to answer the question asked, and then (*d*) condense this information for the reader.

When doing this you should not copy whole sentences unaltered. You may use some of the author's words and you should preserve the order in which information is presented unless this is faulty. However, you must make such changes as are necessary to ensure that in producing your shortened version – the essence of the composition – you do write good English.

Précis writing, as with other questions that require written answers, also tests your vocabulary and spelling, and your ability to write effective sentences and paragraphs in which correct punctuation helps to ensure both clarity and easy reading.

Précis writing skills are important not only (1) in English course work and examinations, when you may be asked to prepare a précis or summary, but also (2) in study (see p. 33), (3) in answering any question which provides information needed in preparing the answer, and (4) in many careers when it is necessary to read documents or other papers, to select information that is needed for a particular purpose, and perhaps to condense this in a report or business letter which, like an examination answer, must be accurate, clear and concise.

Whenever you write you must have a particular reader, or readers, in mind. And you must match your writing to your purpose. You may wish, for example, to persuade, to express sympathy or concern, or to give pleasure. Remember, however, that in a précis you should be conveying another writer's meaning in your own words: you must not therefore add your own opinions or any information that is not in the original composition, and you must not select information for your own purposes in such a way as to present a biased version of the original.

How to prepare a précis
1 Read the instructions carefully to see what you have to do. For example, you may be asked to summarise a composition *in*

your own words as far as possible. You may be told how many words to use.

2   Consider how much time you should spend on this question.

3   Read the composition quickly to see what it is about.

4   Read the composition again slowly to make sure that you understand what each sentence means. If you come across a new word its meaning will probably be obvious from the rest of the sentence or from statements made later.

5   Select a suitable heading or title for your précis.

6   Pick out the topic sentence for each paragraph and use this as a sub-heading, below which you can list the author's main points. The topic sentence states what the paragraph is about (see p. 88) and other sentences in the paragraph give information about this topic.

When you have completed this list of headings and main points, you will have reconstructed the author's topic outline (see p. 130). That is to say, you will have a framework upon which you can construct a summary. In these notes cut out all anecdotes, examples, figurative language, quotations, repetition, and any superfluous words, so that you are left with just the essentials of each paragraph, as in Fig. 7.5.

7   Read the composition again to make sure that your notes do contain the essentials.

8   Now write your précis quickly from your notes. If you are asked to write in your own words this does not mean that you should use none of the writer's words. You must construct effective sentences: you must not simply leave out words so that disconnected words and phrases are strung together. You should not change the author's words just for the sake of changing them: if an author has used the most appropriate word it would be silly to change it just for the sake of replacing it with your own, less appropriate, word.

Usually you will be reporting what another writer has said, and you may therefore be instructed to write in the third person and in the past tense.

9   Count the number of words to make sure that you have not used too many. Note that the number of words required will be indicated in the instructions that are part of the question. To facilitate counting you may arrange your first draft of your

précis in columns with one word in each column (Fig. 7.6).

10 Check your précis against the original composition to make sure that the author is fairly and accurately represented. If necessary, make additions and corrections. Check that the words used in the composition are correctly spelt in your précis. Check that your work reads smoothly and that there are no mistakes in your use of English.

11 If necessary, copy out your corrected précis carefully, so that each word is easy to read (see p. 60), your paragraphs are distinct, and your work as a whole is neatly set out. If your first draft is arranged in columns, for ease in counting, you will not want to present your final version in this form.

12 Write the number of words at the end of your précis.

13 Rule a horizontal line below your précis to indicate that it is complete; and draw a diagonal line through any rough work to indicate that this is not part of your answer.

Exercise 7.6
Read the following extract from Fearns, P. (1984) *Business Studies*, 2nd edn (Sevenoaks, Hodder & Stoughton), and then prepare a précis in under 150 words. (See Figs. 7.5 and 7.6.)

Most people in organisations are specialists. The degree of special skill which is required in a job varies, but it is important to realise that almost everyone in employment is a specialist to some degree. This simply means that in a job we concentrate on specific or specialised tasks – only sole traders perform all the functions in their organisations.

One of the main reasons for the growth in the economy during the nineteenth and twentieth centuries has been the development of specialisation. Specialisation occurs when people, regions or even countries concentrate on what they can do best. Specialisation is common in all organisations and takes place when the total operation is broken down into a series of sub-tasks. The mass production of motor cars provides a good example: in car production hundreds of different components are manufactured separately; the components are then assembled on a production line where each employee performs a repetitive specialist task.

The advantages of specialisation are as follows. (1) People can concentrate on what they are best at. Given the ability, a person can choose to become a secretary or an engineer. (2)

Repetition of the same task increases a person's skill and improves efficiency. (3) Constant employment in the same job can lead to suggestions for improved methods of operation. (4) Breaking operations into sub-routines encourages automation, so that mass production and economies of scale can take place. This advantage is double edged: automation increases productivity and wealth, but at the same time can lead to redundancy and unemployment. Specialisation also creates other disadvantages.

<u>Specialisation</u> means concentrating on a particular kind of work
- almost everyone
- exception = sole traders

<u>Concentrating</u> on what can be done best by individual, region or country.
- reason for economic growth in ⑲th + ⑳th
- break work into smaller tasks

e.g. components of car made by specialists and put together by other specialists

<u>Advantages</u>

<u>Person can</u> (a) choose work according to ability
           (b) develop skill

<u>Employer</u> can benefit from
(a) suggestions from skilled specialists
(b) break-down operation into steps
    facilitates automation, increased
    production and economies of scale.

<u>BUT</u> automation can lead to redundancy and unemployment; and specialisation has other disadvantages.

Fig. 7.5 Rough work: main points of passage set for précis

Specialisation means concentrating on a particular kind of work. specialists: most employees are role, traders being the exception.// Individuals, regions and countries may all concentrate on what they can do best; this is one reason for economic growth in the last two hundred years. Specialisation in any organisation involves breaking work into smaller tasks. For example, the parts of a car are made by different specialists and, * put are specialisation advantages of

The to individuals are

that they can choose

jobs according to ability

and develop skills through

practice. Employers also benefit
_____ 80

from suggestions of skilled

specialists. // The break-down of

an operation into steps

facilitates automation which results
_____ 100

in increased production and

economies of scale, but

can also lead to

redundancy and unemployment. Specialisation

also has other disadvantages
_____ 120

WORDS = 136

Fig. 7.6 Corrected rough draft of précis based on notes of main points (see Fig. 7.5) and arranged in four columns to facilitate counting. // = paragraph break.

Answering comprehension questions

In some questions you are asked to read a short composition and then answer questions that test your understanding (see question 4 on pp. 70–1). To answer such questions you must be able to:

(*a*) concentrate,
(*b*) read carefully,
(*c*) understand each word in context,
(*d*) consider what is being stated or implied,
(*e*) distinguish evidence from unsupported opinion,
(*f*) appreciate the writer's style, and
(*g*) draw conclusions from the information provided.

Your ability to do some or all of these things may be determined by a multiple choice test (as on pp. 70–1). Alternatively, you may be asked to prepare written answers, in which case your ability to prepare effective answers in good English is also tested (see Exercise 7.7).

How to tackle a comprehension question

1 Read any instructions carefully.
2 Read the whole question quickly to see what it is about.
3 Read it again carefully, making sure that you understand what each sentence means. Misreading will result in misunderstanding, and so in wrong answers when you start to write.
4 Time your answers according to the time available (*a*) for the question as a whole, and (*b*) for each part of the question. Answer the questions in the order in which they are set, if you can, but do not spend more time than you can afford on any part that you find difficult: you may have time to come back to this later.
5 Read each part of the questions you have to answer, carefully, to make sure you understand exactly what is required. Do as you are asked, and make sure your answer is complete.
6 If the questions are in the form of a multiple choice test, tackle them as suggested on page 68.
7 If written answers are required, do not just copy a few words from the question paper in the hope that they will suffice. Use your own words to make clear your understanding.

8 If you are told to answer in one word, one phrase, or one sentence, do not write more.

9 If necessary, prepare longer answers in rough work, then correct or otherwise improve them, and then write your answer neatly and legibly in carefully constructed sentences.

10 Check that the parts of your answer are numbered as in the question, and that any words used in the question are spelt correctly. Rule a horizontal line below your answer.

Exercise 7.7

Read the following extract from Miss Read's novel *Gossip from Thrush Green* (Michael Joseph, London). Then answer the questions that follow.

In far too many places in England today, the agreeable habit of taking afternoon tea has vanished.

'Such a shocking waste of time,' says one.

'Much too fattening a meal with all that dreadful
5 starch,' says another.

'Quite unnecessary, if one has had lunch or proposes to eat in the evening,' says a third.

All very true, no doubt, but what a lot of innocent pleasure these strong-minded people are missing! The
10 very ritual of tea-making, warming the pot, making sure that the water is just boiling, inhaling the fragrant steam, arranging the tea-cosy to fit snugly around the precious container, all the preliminaries lead up to the exquisite
15 pleasure of sipping the brew from thin porcelain, and helping oneself to hot buttered scones and strawberry jam, a slice of feather-light sponge cake, or home-made shortbread.

Taking tea is a highly civilised pastime, and fortunately is still in favour at Thrush Green, where it has been
20 brought to a fine art. It is common practice in that pleasant village to invite friends to tea rather than lunch or dinner. As Winnie Bailey, the doctor's widow, pointed out one day to her old friend Ella Bembridge, people could set off from their homes in the light, and return
25 before dark, except for the really miserable weeks of mid-winter when they would probably prefer to stay at home anyway.

1 What are the three reasons given to explain why many people in England no longer take afternoon tea?

2 Why did the doctor's widow prefer to invite people to afternoon tea rather than to lunch or dinner?

3 Write three sentences to show that you understand the meaning of the words *habit* (line 2), *ritual* (line 10), and *preliminaries* (line 13).

4 Decide which is your favourite meal; then briefly explain why.

Notes on your answers to Exercises 7.6 and 7.7

Exercise 7.6 Some people prepare better précis than others, but note that for any précis there is no one right answer and a précis of a passage prepared by you is unlikely to be exactly the same as a précis of the same passage prepared by anyone else.

Exercise 7.7 Comprehension tests of this type could be set in an examination in any subject, not just in English and other language or literature examination papers. In an examination in Physics for example, taken at the age of 18+, you would be able to answer some questions correctly just from the information provided in any comprehension test, but to answer other questions you would have to draw upon your knowledge of Physics from your course work in this subject.

8

Answering Essay-type Questions

This chapter about writing essays and similar compositions includes:
(1) advice on responding to the precise wording of questions and on
using words to convey your thoughts effectively; (2) examples of
different kinds of questions set in course work and examinations,
with specimen answers; and (3) exercises that will cause you to
consider how successful writers plan their compositions – and so help
you to improve your own.

Some of your answers in homework, tests and examinations will
include a number of distinct topics, each of which should be dealt
with in a separate paragraph. For example, you may be asked to
write an essay.

Similar questions, each requiring an organised answer – with a
number of paragraphs arranged in an effective order – begin with
such instructions as: Compare . . . , Contrast . . . , Criticise . . . ,
Describe . . . , Discuss . . . (see Table 8.1). Questions of this type,
in which your answer is given in a number of paragraphs, test your
ability:

1 to **remember** facts and ideas and opinions about one aspect of a
   subject;
2 to **understand** the question and **appreciate** exactly what is
   required for a complete answer;
3 to recall and **consider** information and ideas from different
   sources (to **synthesise**);

4   to **distinguish** relevant from irrelevant material and then **select** enough from what is relevant to answer precisely the question asked;

5   to **display** your knowledge and understanding, to **apply** your knowledge, to **present** an analysis of a situation, to **argue**, or to **evaluate** information provided;

6   to **recognise** distinct parts of a well-balanced answer and then deal with each of them after a suitable heading (if appropriate) and with a separate paragraph for each topic, beginning with an appropriate introductory paragraph and arranging the remaining paragraphs in an appropriate order (the last one being an effective conclusion);

7   to **consider** your purpose and the needs of your reader, so that you can capture and maintain interest, use appropriate language, and write in an appropriate style;

8   to **link** sentences within each paragraph to ensure continuity, and to link paragraphs so that your train of thought is easy to follow and the reader's attention is held;

9   to **spell** correctly;

10   to **choose** words that, with other words in a sentence, convey your meaning precisely;

11   to **arrange** your thoughts simply in correctly punctuated sentences that vary in length, are easy to read, and cannot be misunderstood;

12   to **write appropriately**, according to your purpose, so as to create the impression you intended in the mind of the reader;

13   to **produce** a composition that is original in that the information and ideas presented are selected by you, arranged in your own way, and conveyed in your own words.

In short, in preparing such a composition, you have the opportunity to **display** an educated and lively mind.

Understanding what exactly is required

All essay-type questions test your knowledge of the subject, and your ability to display your understanding, but the examiners' purpose in setting each question (the abilities to be tested and the approach required in your answer) is indicated by the verb used in the question (see Tables 8.1 and 8.2).

Table 8.1 Instructions used in questions testing different
abilities

Purpose of question	*Verbs used in question*
Testing your ability to **remember**	Define
	Describe
	Label
	List
	Outline
	State
Testing your ability to **understand**	Classify
	Explain
	Identify
	Illustrate
	Indicate
Testing your ability to **apply** your knowledge and understanding	Assess
	Change
	Construct
	Demonstrate
	Perform
	Predict
	Relate
	Use
Testing your ability to **analyse**	Analyse
	Calculate
	Criticise
Testing your ability to **synthesise**	Combine
	Construct
	Derive
	Design
	Discuss
Testing your ability to **evaluate**	Clarify
	Evaluate
	Justify
	Select

Every student should realise that apart from lack of knowledge or inability to understand the question, which may make it impossible to prepare a complete answer, the most common reason for under-achievement in course work, tests and examinations is a *failure to answer precisely the question asked.*

This is usually the result of not considering the question suf-ficiently before starting upon an answer, and in particular it is the

Table 8.2 The meanings of verbs used as instructions

Instruction	What you must do
Assess	Judge the worth of.
Compare	Draw attention to similarities between two things, referring also to differences.
Contrast	Draw attention to differences between two things.
Criticise	Judge the merit of, with reasons, including both favourable and unfavourable comments if appropriate.
Describe	Prepare a portrait in words, supplemented if appropriate by diagrams or drawings.
Discuss	Examine by argument, with points for and against an opinion or statement: evidence and opinions.
Evaluate	Judge the value of.
Explain	Account for, or make clear – in detail – to the reader.
Illustrate	Make clear by description, including diagrams if appropriate, or by an example or examples.
Justify	Demonstrate the correctness of.
Outline	Include only the essentials: the main parts.
Relate	Establish the connection between.

Table 8.3 Some words used as instructions in essay-type questions

Verb	Adverb	Noun	Adjective
Describe	briefly concisely	description	brief concise detailed
Explain		explanation account essay	
Assess Criticise Discuss Compare Evaluate Illustrate Justify Relate	critically	assessment critique discussion comparison evaluation illustration justification relation	critical

result of not responding to the words used as instructions. Consider, therefore, the meaning of the verbs listed in Table 8.2 and the meaning of these and other kinds of words included in Table 8.3, all of which are commonly used as instructions in questions and each of which determines the kind of answer you should prepare.

Note particularly that examiners never ask you to 'Write all you know about . . .'. Instead, they make clear exactly what they want to know. It is up to you to consider the meaning of each word used in any question to indicate the *kind* of answer required, as well as exactly what is required. The characteristics of different kinds of answers required in response to different kinds of essay-type questions are summarised in Table 8.4.

Table 8.4 Characteristics of responses to different instructions

Writing exercises	Characteristics of writing
Closed or controlled-response question	
Describe	
Descriptive writing e.g. Describe an object or scene. Proceed from general to particular; from whole to parts; from outside to inside.	Accuracy Clarity Main points plus some detail.
Narrative has an element of description. e.g. Report an event.	Order Simplicity
Explain	
Exposition e.g. Explain how something works. All main aspects plus some details.	Clarity Completeness Conciseness
Discuss	
Discussion/argument Expound views on a subject: evidence; no overstatement. Argue, including points for and against. Strongest argument last. No need to take sides.	Order Accuracy Objectivity Persuasiveness
Open or free-response question	
Essay	
Attempt to deal with a subject as fully as possible, but briefly.	Balance Coherence Relevance

Many questions set in course work and examinations, in all subjects, are *closed* questions (p. 82). In answering them it is not *open* to you to write what you like. You must do exactly what the question asks you to do – but no more.

Answering controlled-response questions

Closed questions are also called *controlled-response questions* because the content of your answer, its arrangement and other characteristics (see Table 8.4) are largely determined or controlled by the precise wording of the question.

Examples of closed or controlled-response questions:

1 **Discuss** the factors which influenced the choice of location for a manufacturing industry you have studied.

2 Most people in the Northern hemisphere eat much more protein each day than the world average daily protein consumption; but in most countries in the Southern hemisphere most people eat much less protein than the world average.

    Either (*a*) Explain these differences in protein consumption.

        Or (*b*) Suggest why many people in some countries are short of food **and** why it is difficult to ensure that all people have an adequate diet.

Comments on Examples

1 The word *discuss* is an instruction. You must include both the advantages and disadvantages of the particular site and draw attention to differences of opinion. It is not enough to simply describe the site or to consider only its advantages.

2 In the second example the word *or* is an instruction. It means that you must not do both. If you do, only (*a*) will be marked. It is not possible to score extra marks by doing more than is required: indeed you will probably lose marks as a result of spending too much time on one question – because you will have less time to spend on the others.

3 The word *and* in 2(*b*) is an instruction. You must do both. In answering such a question, if you do one of the things you are asked to do but not the other you will be answering only part of the question, and showing that you did not understand the question. Obviously, you can score no marks for the part of the question you leave unanswered.

Some closed or controlled-response questions call for what may be called a piece of practical writing in which the arrangement of material, and to some extent the choice of words, is determined by currently accepted practice and by conventions. For example, in English, Communication Studies, and Business Studies examinations, you may be asked to write a letter, and in course work in science subjects you may have to write accounts of investigations.

There are strict conventions in scientific writing, which help the writer in preparing a report on any investigation and help the reader to find the information required in any report. The title indicates what the report is about. This is followed by the name of the person who conducted the investigation, and the name of the laboratory at which the investigation was conducted. The *Introduction* is next: a concise statement of why the work was done. Then the *Materials and Methods* section includes a list of the materials used and the procedures followed so that any reader can see how the work was done, and so that anyone with appropriate facilities can repeat the investigation. The *Results* section indicates what was observed, or calculated from the observations made, and the *Discussion* section is the writer's interpretation of these results in relation to previous investigations concerned with the same problem. Then there may be *Conclusions*, presented as a numbered list. The final part is a list of sources of information or ideas mentioned in the report. This arrangement of material helps to ensure that all the reader's questions are answered: What? Where? When? How? Why? Who? And this is why scientists always write in this way, whether they are pupils studying science subjects at school, students at college, or working scientists writing accounts of their work for publication.

Exercise 8.1   Prepare an answer to this controlled-response question based on your notes (see the plan in Fig. 8.1). The specimen answer (Fig. 8.2) shows how your letter could be arranged.

Write a letter, properly laid out, in which you apply for an advertised vacancy. Address your letter to the Personnel Manager. State the vacancy for which you are applying and when and where you saw it advertised. State your age, where you went to school, and details of any examination results. If you are studying, say what course you are taking, when your results will be known, and when you will be available for employment if selected. Refer to your non-academic interests and any achievements which may set you apart from other applicants. Say when you could attend for interview.

Draw attention, particularly, to your reason for applying for this work (e.g. why you think you would find the work interesting and worthwhile) and why you think you could make a success of the job. Give the names and addresses of two people who would be prepared to support your application by giving information about your character and achievements.

Post applied for:
Where advertised:
Age:
School:

Subjects studied at school and examination results:

Present course:
Subjects studied:

Date results expected:
Date available to start work:
Part time and vacation work undertaken:

Non-academic interests and any achievements:

Reasons for applying for this post:

Names of two referees:

Fig. 8.1   Notes of things that should be included in your application

Your address here

Date

The Personnel Manager
Name and
address of
employer

Dear Sir,

Name of position applied for

Please consider this application for the above post, advertised in
.... on .... I am keen to make a career in
.... and the work described in
your advertisement is very similar to work I have undertaken as part
of my course in .... at ....
....

I am .... years of age and went to ....
.... school, where my grades in the
.... examinations were as follows.

....
....
....
....
....

Since leaving school I have worked part-time as a ....
.... for ....
and studied ....
at ....
My final examinations will be in .... and I should
therefore be available for employment at the end of ....

Mr .... , my Headmaster at ....
....
and Mr .... , owner of ....
where I have worked part-time since .... , have said that
they would be pleased to support this application.

Yours faithfully,

Fig. 8.2 Specimen application (see Exercise 8.1)

Exercise 8.2   Make a list of the topics for paragraphs, and a note of the thoughts that should be expressed in each paragraph, in answer to this controlled-response question:

Outline, briefly, the basic principles of food hygiene.

Note: The word *outline* indicates that only main points are required (no detail, explanation or examples) and the word *brief* indicates that your answer must be as short as possible.

Specimen list of topics, and notes for an answer to this question

List of topics for paragraphs	*Information and ideas relevant to each paragraph*
Food in shops	Work surfaces and serving utensils should be kept clean and sterile. Uncooked meats and cooked meats should not be kept together. Serving utensils used for one should not be used for the other. Food should be wrapped to keep cooked and uncooked food apart and to keep food clean.
Food preparation	Fresh fruit and vegetables should be washed. Clean water and clean utensils should be used for all food preparation.
Cooking food	Food should be sufficiently cooked to kill any bacteria. Re-heated meat dishes should be boiled for at least twenty minutes.
Food storage	Perishable foods, especially cooked foods, should be properly stored to prevent the growth and multiplication of bacteria and fungi. Deep-frozen foods once thawed should not be re-frozen. Foods should not be kept for more than a few days in a domestic refrigerator.
Personal hygiene	People handling, preparing and serving food should have clean hands and clean clothing, and should wash their hands after blowing their nose or going to the lavatory.

Exercise 8.3 Outline, briefly, the basic principles of food hygiene. Base your answer on the plan prepared in Exercise 8.2.

Specimen answer

Hygiene is the study of the principles of healthy living; and food hygiene means keeping food clean and uncontaminated by disease-producing organisms – at all stages in preparation and processing, and in distribution, storage, handling and sale.

Food offered for sale should be covered to exclude insects and rodents, and so that people cannot breathe or cough on it, or it should be inside clean display cabinets or closed packages. It is especially important that un-cooked meats, which may be contaminated with harmful bacteria, should not be kept near to cooked meats. Also, to prevent cross-contamination, utensils used for displaying, cutting or serving one food should not also be used for another. All utensils and working surfaces should be kept clean and all food sold should be properly wrapped to keep it clean in the shopping basket, and to prevent different foods coming into contact with one another.

Clean water and utensils should be used for all food preparation; and fresh fruit and vegetables should be washed before they are served at the table or used in kitchens. When food is first cooked it should be sufficiently cooked to kill any bacteria; and re-heated meat dishes – which are a common cause of food poisoning – should be boiled for at least twenty minutes to destroy both the bacteria themselves and the toxins they produce.

Perishable foods, especially cooked foods, should be eaten fresh or properly stored. At the temperature of a domestic refrigerator most foods can be kept for only a few days because of fungi that cause food spoilage, and bacteria that cause food spoilage and food poisoning. Deep-frozen foods, once thawed, should not be re-frozen because bacteria multiply at higher temperatures and are not killed by subsequent lower temperatures.

To reduce the chances of contamination, food hygiene must be maintained by all those concerned at every stage in food processing and food handling. All people preparing, selling, serving or eating food should have clean clothing and clean hands. They should not cough or sneeze on food and should wash their hands after using a handkerchief or using the lavatory, because there may be harmful bacteria on their hands – as on the filthy feet of faecal-feeding flies.

Specimen marking scheme

	Marks
Introduction: what is food hygiene?	2
Keeping food clean in shops, in shopping basket and in home	4
Cleanliness of utensils for food preparation, storage and serving	4
Cooked foods; re-heated foods and food poisoning	4
Personal hygiene of all food handlers	4
Conclusion	2
Total =	20

Notes on Exercises 8.2 and 8.3
It is helpful to consider, in planning answers, how the question is likely to be marked. However, you will not *know* the examiners' marking scheme. Your answer, therefore, is unlikely to be set out exactly as in the marking scheme but it should include all the main points – for which marks will be given.

Business writing and scientific writing are brief and concise: information and ideas are conveyed without ornament. This is the economical writing that is well suited to scoring marks quickly in the short time that is available in examinations. Unfortunately, however, instruction in composition in schools is usually given mainly by teachers of English who, in association with the study of literature, devote most time to teaching imaginative writing. This is the language of the novel and the English essay, which are concerned not with presenting information and ideas in a straightforward way but with painting pictures in the mind. As a result, many pupils learn to write a reasonable English essay (a free-response) and yet are not so well equipped for writing the clear and simple English required in answering the controlled-response questions set in course work and examinations in other subjects.

Answering free-response questions

An English essay is an example of the kind of answer required in a free-response or open-ended question. Open in this context means that it is open to you to decide what should be included in your answer, and how it should be arranged. In contrast with the closed or controlled-response questions considered on pages 116–22, the information required is not stated in the question. The way you respond will depend more on your personal experiences and feelings, but as in any other composition a balanced answer is always required and only relevant material should be included.

Examples of open-ended or free-response questions

1 Write a story that begins with the words: The best fairy stories are written for adults, read to children, and enjoyed by both.

2 Use this poem as the starting point for a piece of imaginative writing (not a poem) in which you express your own feelings after some experience that made you think afresh about your own life or your attitude to other people.

> *Afterthoughts*
> Lonely the wind that falls to hollow:
> Sweetest hearts rest in the grave.
> Only thoughts live. Calm may follow,
> After the breaking of the wave.
>
> Only thoughts live for tomorrow,
> In the lives of kith and kin.
> Spreading ripples, fading sorrow:
> Sweetest thoughts where hearts have been.

3 Look at a picture of people in your daily newspaper or in a magazine. Do not read the caption to the picture or the report about it. Instead, write your own story – based *either* on what you see in the picture *or* solely on the train of thought the picture evokes.

In contrast to a controlled-response question in which all students' answers should have many things in common, corresponding to all aspects of a good answer included in the examiners' marking scheme (for example, see p. 122), in a free-response question all answers might be expected to be different. As the term free-response indicates, in answering these questions there is most scope for individuality. Marks are awarded for an appropriate selection of material, for the use of appropriate language, for good English, and for the effect of your writing upon the reader (the examiner).

Style in writing depends upon the writer, the writer's purpose, and the needs of the reader. You may benefit in many ways from preparing any communication, but your purpose is always to inform or to affect the reader in a chosen way.

Exercise 8.4   To help you achieve your purpose in any composition, consider how carefully professional writers put words together in different kinds of writing.

Descriptive writing: painting a picture in words of a person, an object, or a scene.

From the summit of the island we searched the seemingly dead landscape with field-glasses. On every side the water stretched away to the horizon, broken here and there by splits of still-dry mud, scattered bulrush stubble, and an occasional dense reed-bed. It was a landscape of two colours, the pale diffident blue of sky and water broken only by the drab of mud-reach and reed. It was strange how empty and lifeless this composition appeared to the naked eye, and how teeming it became through the lenses.
A Reed Shaken by the Wind   Gavin Maxwell (1957)

Narrative: describing an occurrence or an event.

The soldier gaped. He saluted, still looking doubtful, and began to walk up the side of the moat towards the wicket-gate. We did not look back but hastened up to the path on the far side, and, passing the married quarters, came to the high oak paling which bordered the pathway above the park. We were still within the faint glare of searchlights. Every moment that we stayed on the pathway was dangerous. Lifting ourselves quickly over the paling, we landed in thick snow among the tangle of trees.
They Have Their Exits   Airey Neave (1953)

Imaginative writing: based wholly or in part on the imagination.

The real evils, indeed, of Emma's situation were the power of having rather too much of her own way, and a disposition to think a little too well of herself: these were the disadvantages which threatened alloy to her many enjoyments. The danger, however, was at present so unperceived, that they did not by any means rank as misfortunes with her.
Emma   Jane Austen (1816)

In imaginative writing words are chosen to paint vivid pictures and evoke particular emotions in the reader's mind. Adjectives (e.g. white) and adverbs (e.g. easily) are used as well as the nouns (e.g. horse, fence) and verbs (e.g. jumped) needed for plain statements. Instead of 'The horse jumped the fence', you could write: 'The white horse jumped the fence easily.' This would give the reader a much clearer picture.

Answering the question: composition

Preparing to write a composition

In a composition you put your thoughts together and present them for a reader. To inform and interest this reader you must write about things that you know and understand – which you find interesting yourself.

First read the question carefully: ask yourself what each word means. Why has it been included in the question? When you are quite sure that you understand what it is, exactly, that the examiner wants to know, consider your answer.

Think about each word in the question and make notes of relevant ideas that come to mind. Spread these notes over a whole page; perhaps using some words from the question as headings. This is your rough work – a record of your accumulating thoughts.

Arrange these thoughts in a way that you find, by experience, suits you best. Some people find that making a diagram is a stimulus to thinking. For example, if you were asked to write an essay on flowers, you could write the essay title in the centre of a sheet of paper (as in Fig. 8.3). Draw a line around this title. As you think of things that might be included in your composition, make notes around the edge of the page – under appropriate headings and with each heading connected to the essay title by a line.

Another way to arrange your thoughts, as you think about any question, is to record the title at the top of a sheet of paper (as in Fig. 8.4). Then list your main points as headings with space below each heading. As you are doing this, points that should be included in an explanation, supporting details, and suitable examples, can be noted below each heading in the most appropriate place.

Making yourself think

When you have to answer any free-response question, one way to jog your memory is to consider the different subjects you are studying and your non-academic interests. For example, in thinking about flowers in an English examination you might consider:

English language: How are flowers named?

English literature: What books and poems have you read in which flowers are mentioned?

History: Have flowers been used as emblems in the history of your country? What about other countries?

Geography: Are particular kinds of flowering plants grown as crop plants in different countries? What is their economic importance?

Biology: What is a flower?

Chemistry: Which perfumes come from flowers?

Art and design: How have flowers been represented?

Gardening?

A second way to jog your memory, instead of thinking about the different subjects you have studied, is to think about different aspects of one subject. For example, if an essay question on flowers were set in a Biology examination, you would consider:

Plant physiology: Why do different kinds of plants flower at different times of the year?

Plant ecology: What kinds of flowering plants grow in different kinds of soils? What kinds of plants grow together?

Plant structure: What are the parts of a flower?

Plant reproduction: What is the function of each part of a flower?

A third way to remind yourself of things that might be included in any composition is to ask yourself these one-word questions:

What?   Where?   When?   How?   Why?   Who?

For example, if you were asked to write about houses, these questions should help you to make notes of relevant points that might be included in your composition:

What is a house?

Where are houses built?

When did people start building houses?

How are houses constructed? *What* materials are used?

Why do people build houses?

Who lives in houses? Do all people live in them?

A Thinking

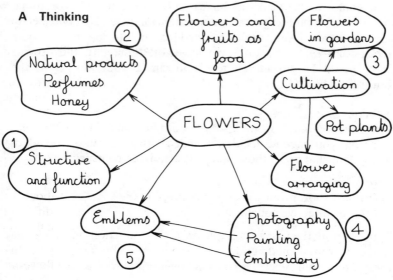

B Planning

1   Flower structure and function

2   Economic importance of flowers

3   Growing flowers for decoration

4   Flowers as a source of inspiration in art
    and literature (poetry)

5   Flowers in history and politics
    Flower as a message, in itself, in emblem or
    in popular song.

Fig. 8.3   Thinking about an essay on flowers and planning the composition

In course work you do not have to rely, as you would in examinations, solely on things you can remember. Indeed, it is a good idea to look at your textbook, and at other sources of information and ideas (see pp. 23–8), to check that you have noted correctly all the points that should be considered for inclusion in your answer to the question asked.

Selecting and arranging
After making notes of things that could be included in your composition, you have to decide (1) which topics should be included, and (2) in what order they should be arranged to ensure:

(*a*)   an effective beginning,
(*b*)   an appropriate order of paragraphs, and
(*c*)   an effective conclusion.

In an essay the first paragraph is your introduction, in which you make clear that you do understand the question by starting straight away upon your answer. You may even give the essence of your answer in this first paragraph.

There will then be further paragraphs (usually four, five or six, depending partly on the wording of the question and partly in an examination on the time available), with each paragraph occupying about a quarter to a half page of writing. This should help to stop you writing too much about one aspect of your answer (one topic) when you should be trying to give a balanced answer by devoting a similar amount of time to each aspect – if these are equal in importance.

Number the headings in your rough work (as in Figs 8.3 and 8.4) to indicate how the paragraphs can be arranged in an effective order. In some answers this will be the order of the parts of the question (e.g. in your answers to most controlled-response questions). In other answers the only appropriate order may be that in which events occurred. In a description it may be the order in which parts are arranged. In other answers an effective order may be world region by world region, or country by country. When you have decided on the topics to be included in your answer, and decided how to begin, a suitable order for the remaining paragraphs will probably be obvious to you.

Order is important in mathematics and in science subjects, in

B Planning | A Thinking

1	House a shelter: one or more rooms. Use of rooms for different purposes
6	House as a basis for family life — more than a shelter.
3	Suitable situations for building — growth of settlements
2	Houses in different countries materials used climate
4	What were the first houses like?
5	Houses today – some similar to those built thousands of years ago; some very different Future?
7	Forming a picture of life in the past from foundations of houses and archaelogical remains. House and belongings a record of the way people lived.

Order of paragraphs | **Topics for paragraphs**

Fig. 8.4 Thinking about houses and planning a composition on this subject. Note that numbering the topics for paragraphs (planning) comes after thinking, when you order your material.

arranging steps in your working that lead to a solution, and order is necessary in any writing (see Table 8.5). Successive paragraphs should lead the reader, step by step, to your last one – which is your conclusion. In most subjects the examiner will give marks for relevant information and ideas included in each paragraph. Your last paragraph, therefore, should not be a summary: you cannot expect to score extra marks for repeating the main points from paragraphs that have already been marked. To gain more and more marks, in each paragraph you must add to what has gone before.

Table 8.5   Comparing different kinds of answer: the need for order

Problem solving	*Preparing a written answer*
1 Think about the problem.	Think about the question.
2 Arrange working in order.	Arrange paragraphs in order.
3 Underline answer.	Write an effective conclusion.

Preparing to write a composition is rather like gathering the materials needed to construct a building. Instead of gathering all the components in one large heap, you would make separate heaps for each type of component, or arrange for materials to be delivered in separate batches so that you could start with the foundation, then build the rooms, and end with the roof. In a composition you arrange your materials so that it is easy to write an introduction that provides a good beginning (a firm foundation), separate paragraphs for separate topics (arranged in order like the rooms of a building and with suitable connections between them), and end with an effective conclusion that adds something useful and completes your work (like the roof of a building).

As you prepare your plan or *topic outline* for a composition, it is as well to consider what the examiner will be looking for in an answer to this particular question. Appropriate language and style are always required (e.g. standard English, formal or more familiar, but not colloquial language or slang). Also, as in marking short written answers (see p. 82), the examiner will have a marking scheme which includes certain topics – and will be looking to see if you have included each of these topics, with enough explanation in each paragraph not only to display your knowledge of a topic but also to make clear your understanding.

Drawing diagrams

In most subjects, but not in English or other language examinations, diagrams should be included in written answers if they are needed as part of any explanation. Such diagrams must be simple so that they can be drawn quickly but neatly. They should be placed at the most appropriate point in your answer (not all together at the end), and each one should be clearly labelled to draw attention to things that are relevant to the particular question you are answering. Do not include diagrams just for ornament.

Because a diagram is included, fewer words than would otherwise be needed should be used in your explanation. In this way, drawing the diagram should save you time. You should refer to the diagram in your writing but you do not have time, especially in examinations, to convey the same information in both pictures and words. What is more, remember that examiners do not like to be told the same things twice.

Writing a composition

The length of your composition may be limited by the time available (as in an examination). If not, however long you spend on thinking, seeking information and ideas, and planning, always try to *write* each composition in the length of time that would be available for it in an examination.

In an English examination, taken at the age of sixteen or later, with an hour for the whole composition, you might well spend ten to fifteen minutes preparing your answer, forty to forty-five minutes writing no more than 600 words (two to three pages on wide-lined A4 paper), and five minutes checking your work. In course work you could spend more time on preparation but you should still write an answer of about the same length, and in about the same time – even if you then spend more time on checking and improving your work. In course work you should also be prepared to rewrite your answer, converting a first draft into a more polished composition.

Most professional writers do this. With practice in preparing and writing, and criticising your own work instead of waiting for a teacher to make corrections and to suggest improvements, your writing will improve and in examinations you will be better able to write a good first draft that needs only careful checking and minor corrections.

In all subjects it is worth thinking about the question and then planning your answer, instead of spending all the time writing, because marks are given for what you write – for the content and quality of your work – not for the use of more words than are needed for a competent answer to the question set.

Following your plan

When you write, follow your plan. This will enable you to (1) write quickly (but remember that each word must be legible); (2) write an effective introduction; (3) arrange your answer for easy marking by using effective headings, if appropriate, and by clear indentation at the start of each new paragraph; (4) deal with all aspects of the question set and ensure continuity in each paragraph; (5) keep each paragraph short and to the point; (6) arrange your paragraphs in order and link them effectively; (7) avoid repetition; and (8) ensure that anything irrelevant is omitted.

In short, your plan helps you to avoid producing a verbose, repetitive, rambling and incoherent composition that fails to capture and hold the interest of the reader. Examiners see far too much of this kind of writing and are agreeably surprised and impressed when they come across a well organised and carefully laid out composition.

In course work refer to your textbook and to other sources of information if you need them, to help you with your planning, and then put them on one side. Instead of copying sentences from books it is usually best to work with only your plan as a guide. In this way you can choose words that form an answer to precisely the question asked, and you can show that instead of copying someone else's words you have thought about the question, understood what is required, and chosen words to convey your own thoughts.

Using words effectively

As you write, use appropriate language (see p. 56) and use only words that you understand. Prefer a short word to a long one unless the long word is needed to convey your meaning more precisely. Do not use long words just in an attempt to impress the reader.

Exercise 8.5
Suggest a short word that could be used instead of each of the
following long words:
1   additional
2   commence
3   fabricate
4   hypothesise
5   importantly
6   personnel
7   proceed
8   utilisation

Suggested answers
(1) extra,   (2) begin,   (3) build,   (4) suggest,
(5) important,   (6) people,   (7) go,   (8) use.

Comment
Note when other people use long words unnecessarily. This will help you to
avoid making the same mistake.

Try not to use more words than are needed to convey your
thoughts and to make proper connections between these thoughts.
Unnecessary words will hinder your reader's progress and so make
communication more difficult than it would have been had these
extra words been omitted.

If any words can be left out without altering the meaning of a
sentence it is usually best to do without them. Every word in your
compositions should be included to convey information or ideas, or
to affect the reader in a chosen way. No words should be added just
to make a little knowledge go a long way. You do not want to give
the impression that you are short of relevant things to include in
your answers. Examiners are likely to be annoyed at having to waste
time on reading mere padding; and they are unlikely to be fooled by
such verbal decorations.

Professor C. A. Mace in *The Psychology of Study* gave this
advice:

> There are many styles of window dressing, and many ways of
> being a plausible rogue in the formal examination as in the
> other tests of life. But . . . examiners . . . have had, as a rule,
> more experience in defending themselves against these devices

than the most practised student has had in employing them. But . . . is it not more reasonable to regard the examination not as a duel but as a species of cooperation? The examiner is not concerned to expose the bottomless pits of ignorance in the student's mind . . . He is interested rather in the little hills of erudition which also diversify the scenery of an otherwise even plain. In this inquiry he relies in the last resort upon the student to help him. The student can help best not by endeavouring to conceal the pits but by drawing attention with a measure of pardonable pride to the presence of the little hills.

Exercise 8.6
Without altering the meaning of each of the following items, suggest which words should be deleted:
1   actual facts
2   completely surrounded
3   deliberately avoided
4   equal halves
5   genuinely sorry
6   green in colour
7   link together
8   real problems
9   rectangular in shape
10   very true

Answers
(1) actual, (2) completely, (3) deliberately, (4) equal, (5) genuinely, (6) in colour, (7) together, (8) real, (9) in shape, (10) very.

Note: (1) Words with only one meaning should not be qualified. For example, all problems are real and rectangular is a shape.

(2) Saying the same thing twice, using different words, makes clear to the reader that you do not know the meaning of the words you have used, and is called *tautology*. For example, 'link' means 'put together'.

Exercise 8.7
Make a note of one word that could be used instead of each of the following phrases:
1   at this precise moment in time
2   at an early date
3   it may well be that
4   make an adjustment to

5 undertake a study of
6 have a listen
7 four in number
8 continuing to progress

Answers
(1) now, (2) soon, (3) perhaps, (4) adjust,
(5) study, (6) listen, (7) four, (8) progressing.

Note that one word should always be preferred to a phrase unless the phrase makes your meaning clearer or makes for easier reading.

Also, when possible, be precise. Instead of *soon*, state when. Instead of *many*, state how many.

It is particularly important to make the first words of each sentence do useful work. And use the first words of each paragraph to make an immediate impression on the reader. If they indicate what the paragraph is to be about, it will not usually be necessary to use extra words just to make the connection between this paragraph and the last one. The train of thought will be obvious to the reader.

To help your readers, and so help yourself to score marks in course work, tests and examinations, you are advised to proceed as follows:

1 Plan your work.
2 Use a separate paragraph for each part of your answer, and mark the start of each paragraph by clear indentation.
3 Use words to convey and not to conceal your meaning.

Padding is likely to indicate gaps in your knowledge. Therefore, concentrate on scoring marks for what you know. Without the obstacles to efficient communication provided by unnecessary words, your teachers and examiners will not need to search for relevant information and so will find it easier to award marks. In each paragraph:

(*a*) make your point,
(*b*) give enough supporting detail to display your knowledge,
(*c*) give enough explanation, and perhaps an example, to show your understanding, and
(*d*) bring this aspect of your answer to an end in such a way that the reader is led smoothly to the next.

Exercise 8.8

Suggest how each of the following items could (and therefore should) be expressed more clearly in fewer words:

1   The report is in its final stages of completion.
2   They were almost identical to each other.
3   In conclusion I think it is fair to say that . . .
4   Thus there is a definite need to bring about a reduction in the amount of malnutrition from which approximately one-quarter of the world's population suffer.

Suggested rewording

1   The report is almost complete.
2   They were almost identical.
3   Omit all such padding, especially at the start of a paragraph where important words should be placed – to catch the eye and the attention of the reader.
4   Thus there is a need to reduce (or prevent?) the malnutrition from which perhaps a quarter of all people suffer.

The use of more words than are needed to convey meaning effectively is called *circumlocution*. Check each of your own compositions to see if you can find words that should be deleted, or thoughts that could be communicated more effectively in fewer words.

Reading compositions by successful authors, for pleasure, will help you to appreciate the weight of appropriate words suitably arranged (*a*) in effective sentences, and (*b*) in well ordered paragraphs.

Looking carefully and critically at any composition, as a comprehension exercise (see p. 70 and p. 109), will not only test your understanding of the work but also help you to see how other people explain things and how carefully they select and arrange words to convey their meaning precisely or to make a particular impression upon the reader.

Successful authors check their writing to see if they can improve it, for example by removing any unnecessary words, before allowing anyone else to see their compositions. Read one paragraph in any well-known book by an established writer, or any lines from any poem in a book of verse, to see if there is a word that could be omitted without losing something in the way of meaning or atmosphere or coherence. For example, see Exercise 6.4 on pages 88–90.

Keeping to the point

Studying any composition before writing a summary or précis, or before making notes, helps you to distinguish the topic for each paragraph from the supporting details, to recognise superfluous words, and to appreciate the uses of figurative language.

Practice in planning and writing your own compositions helps you to think about your purpose, to decide what is necessary to fulfil this purpose, to arrange this material in paragraphs (with one topic for each paragraph and only necessary detail), to discard irrelevant thoughts that come to mind, and to present your thoughts in an effective order.

Whereas in writing a précis or summary, or in making notes, you start with a composition (see Table 8.6), in writing your own composition you start with notes – with an annotated summary or topic outline (see Table 8.7).

Recognising good and bad in other people's writing, including well ordered and badly ordered material, and relevance and irrelevance, should help you to improve your own compositions.

Table 8.6 Preparing notes, a summary, or a précis

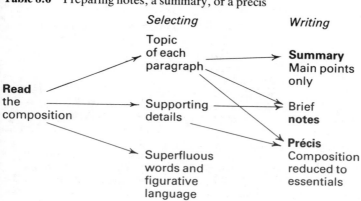

Table 8.7 Preparing a composition

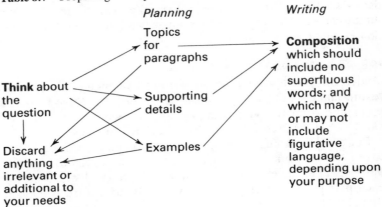

Table 8.8 What your marks mean

Mark out of 10	Comments
10	Outstanding
8+	Excellent
	Neat, properly laid out for easy reading, and easy to understand. All parts relevant and the whole well balanced, with enough attention to each aspect, with enough explanation and, where appropriate, with examples.
6+	Good
	With few or no mistakes in the use of English; neat work. Lack of balance may result from too much attention to some topics and not enough to others. Some points may be insufficiently explained.
4+	Mistakes in the use of English may interfere with communication. Omissions or the inclusion of irrelevant material may indicate lack of knowledge or an inability to distinguish relevant from irrelevant information.
	Lower marks indicate lack of knowledge of the subject or an inability to organise an effective composition that answers the question asked.

So that you can do better work, consider what teachers are looking for when they assess students' compositions (see Table 8.8). It is best to make corrections yourself, if you can, so that you do not lose marks when teachers and examiners correct your work.

Checking your composition
Delete any rough work with one diagonal line; and then check your composition.

1 Have you answered all parts of the question, and is each part clearly sign-posted?
2 Have all points in your plan been included in your answer?
3 Can you find any slips of the pen or other obvious mistakes?
4 Is every word legible and does your composition read well?
5 Can you find any faults in spelling, punctuation or grammar?
6 Except in an examination, when the date will be written on the front cover of your answer book, always remember to put your name and the date *on everything you write*.

PART THREE

Revision and Examination Techniques

Many students keep up to date, from week to week, but in doing so neglect previous work. In Part Three both long-term and short-term preparations for examinations are considered, and advice is given on both revision and examination techniques.

9

Revising for Tests and Examinations

This chapter will help you to use the syllabus for your course as a guide to the scope of your studies and to the aspects you may be questioned upon in course work, in progress or phase tests, and in the examinations taken at the end of your course. Revision techniques are recommended (1) for use as part of study throughout your course, and (2) to help you prepare in the weeks immediately preceding your examinations.

What must you study?

What you will need to study, to do well in course work and in the examinations you plan to take at the end of your course, is summarised in the syllabus for each subject printed in the regulations for these examinations.

Alternatively, instead of a syllabus, you may be given a set of learning objectives: a statement of the things you should be able to do as a result of your studies. Your ability to do these things may then be tested in both your course work and in examinations.

If you are studying at school or college, or taking a correspondence course, your teachers will be helping you to prepare for a particular examination. They should have studied the requirements of the examiners before planning a course that is suited to your needs, but you can still benefit from looking at the regulations yourself.

Knowing what your course comprises, from the beginning, will help you to see each subject as a whole. This will give direction to your studies: from week to week you will be able to see how the course is developing, what has been done, and what has still to be done.

The syllabus is especially important if you are working without a teacher. On the one hand, a textbook is likely to include more topics than any one syllabus (because of the need to provide for different students working to the syllabuses of different examination boards). On the other hand, a textbook may not include all the topics in a particular syllabus: you may have to use more than one book to provide a sound basis for your study of some subjects – especially if you are not attending classes.

Look at the syllabus for your course again each time you start to study a new aspect of the subject, to remind yourself of what the examiners consider most important. Then look at the syllabus and your notes, yet again, after studying this aspect of your work and before moving on to the next – to check that you have done all that is necessary at this stage. Check particularly that you have completed the necessary work and have understood it.

It is a good idea to emphasise words from the syllabus in your notes, for example by (1) copying out extracts from the syllabus at the beginning of each aspect of your studies, and (2) marking these words in your notes by underlining them in a different colour (perhaps green) that stands out from the black or blue/black ink you use for writing and from the red ink used by most teachers for corrections and for comments on your work.

Your preparations for tests and examinations will be similar. For both, you are advised to revise all aspects of your subject upon which you may be questioned. In tests made up of short-answer or objective test questions, all aspects of the syllabus may be covered and you may be asked to answer all questions – so the more you know about the subject the more questions you should be able to attempt and the more marks you should be able to score. And in examinations in which you have a choice of questions, from which to select those you can answer best, obviously the more questions you could answer the greater your choice. You are therefore advised not to restrict your choice by studying and revising only part of the material included in the syllabus for your course.

How will you be judged?

With large classes it is difficult for teachers to set regular essay-type questions for homework, because marking long answers would take too long. Progress or phase tests may therefore be set, at regular intervals, to monitor your progress. This is necessary if teachers are to assess the effectiveness of their teaching; and it is necessary for you to know how well you are doing and where further work is needed. In some courses regular tests and homework are marked to assess performance, and these marks are used – in addition to or instead of final examinations – in determining your grades for your course.

Whereas course work is usually marked by your teachers, your final examination may be set and marked by external examiners. It may seem fair to judge students by their performance throughout a course rather than by the standard of work produced on one day in one examination. This is to the advantage of any student who is not feeling well on the day of an examination or who, because of poor examination technique, does not know how to use the time effectively in an examination.

Two disadvantages of continuous assessment, however, are that work completed in a student's own time may not be entirely that student's own work – and there is a possibility of favouritism or victimisation. A third disadvantage is that students who maintain the same standard throughout the course (good, satisfactory or poor) have little to gain or lose from an assessment based on an average mark, whereas the weak student who improves steadily and reaches a peak at the end of the course – as a result of sustained effort and perhaps also effective teaching – may obtain a lower grade than would have been achieved had the assessment been based entirely upon the standard of work done at the end of the course.

A fourth disadvantage of continuous assessment is that each piece of course work is set not only to help the student but also as a means of assessment. That is to say, teaching and assessment – which should be separate – become confused. The whole purpose of teaching, supported by course work, should be to help students to think and to learn. Obviously, as a student, you should know how you will be judged: this knowledge will affect your attitude

to your teachers and your approach to course work and examinations.

Rules for learning

Attempts to understand learning are central in psychology, the
study of human behaviour, but no one knows what happens when
we learn. There are probably as many opinions as there are psychologists! No one can provide a magic formula that will help you to
learn. The advice on learning given in this chapter is therefore to
help you to find ways of learning that suit you best.

In first examinations, taken at the age of 16+, some marks can be
scored for things remembered parrot-fashion – without understanding. In answering some questions, all that is necessary is to mention
points included in the examiners' marking scheme: marks will then
be given even if it is clear from the context that the work is not fully
understood. This may encourage some teachers to devote too much
time to teaching facts, and cause some pupils to think that to study
means to memorise answers to questions that may be set in examinations. This is unfortunate because to answer most questions it is
necessary to understand as well as to remember, and it is not usually
possible to score good marks by relying on the memory alone.

Furthermore, pupils who devote their study time to memorising
notes are unlikely to find their work interesting and they will not be
well prepared for the kind of study that is essential if they go on
to take a more advanced course in preparation for higher-level
examinations.

Things remembered without understanding may be soon forgotten. It is better to base your learning on study techniques that will
contribute to your understanding, and to the development of your
interest in all aspects of the course. In the following rules for
learning, therefore, little attention is paid to techniques for remembering things parrot-fashion.

1 Know why you wish to learn

The most common reason for failure to achieve one's full potential
in study, as in most things, is lack of motivation. The student who
does not have the desire to learn, who does not really want to know,
is unlikely to make the most of any opportunity to learn.

You are likely to do your best work throughout any course of study and in examinations if you are working to some purpose. This may be a desire to know more about certain subjects, just out of curiosity, or to do as well as possible in examinations, or to enter upon or obtain promotion in a particular career.

Therefore, consider your reasons for studying. You will find it easiest to remember things that you have a reason for remembering: you will find it easiest to learn if you really do *want* to know and understand.

2 Study things that you find interesting

You will probably score good marks in course work and obtain high grades in examinations in those subjects you find most interesting. One reason for this is that you will find it easy to attend to anything that needs to be done.

It is important, therefore, to maintain and develop your interest in your chosen subjects. You can do this, if you have an enquiring mind, by always seeking answers to the questions that come to mind. In teaching yourself to think, as you observe, listen or read, ask yourself questions:

How is this known?
Can it be so?
What is the evidence for this?
What follows from this, if it is correct?

Try to find answers to your questions. Your search for further information will add interest to your studies. Your curiosity will be rewarded with a better understanding.

The more you understand, the better you will know what you need to remember, and the easier it will be to retain and recall these most important points.

3 Survey the whole before you study its parts

Consider the subjects you are studying, connections between these subjects, and the scope of each subject.

Look at the syllabus or learning objectives for your course so that you can see how each week's work fits into the course as a whole. Similarly, view any book quickly and as a whole, by looking at the contents pages and by skim-reading, before you study its parts.

Then, in studying selected pages, first read quickly to see the author's purpose and how the material is arranged. In this way you prepare yourself for a second, more careful, reading, for preparing a précis or summary, or for making notes.

In these, and in other aspects of study, try to start with an awareness of the whole. A plan provides a framework for your study of the parts, and is especially important when there is a definite structure to the material you are studying. Being aware of the whole will help you to see connections between the parts as your studies proceed. And when you have studied all the parts you will be able to view the whole in a new light.

4   Get things right the first time

Listen carefully. Read carefully. Make sure that you understand things before deciding what you need to remember. Ask questions when there are things you do not follow or cannot understand. It is easiest to learn if you can get things right the first time you study them. If you do not, it may prove difficult to discard your early misunderstandings and misconceptions. At first you will not be aware of them. Then you will have to appreciate where you went wrong, correct your mistakes, and unlearn – replacing misunderstanding with understanding.

5   Concentrate on one task at a time

Having recognised different tasks that need your attention (see p. 37), and having numbered them in your order of priority (see p. 44), you will find it easiest to learn if your mind is occupied in study with one task at a time.

In a two- or three-hour study session you might then tackle two or three distinct tasks – one at a time. You may also find it best to work at different subjects so that you receive encouragement from your progress in one even though you may be struggling and trying to overcome some difficulty in another.

Working at different kinds of subjects in successive study periods will also reduce the chances of your study of one subject interfering with your study of another: for example, you might find it confusing if you started to learn two languages and worked at them both on the same evening.

6 Keep your notes on each subject in good order

In a well organised course your teacher may begin by saying how the subject will be taught. This course outline will help you to see the connection between one class and the next, and to understand why topics are being taught in a particular sequence.

Similarly, in class, your teacher can help you by making logical connections between topics and also by well reasoned argument.

You will find your notes easier to understand, and you will learn more, if you are always aware of an organised sequence in your studies and can keep the notes on each subject separately and in good order.

Your teacher may provide lesson plans, maps, diagrams, flow charts or tables. These may serve as summaries and help you to see patterns, sequences and connections. They will make learning easier. And if your teacher does not help you in this way, you may find similar learning aids in your textbook, or you can help yourself by preparing suitable summaries at the end of each piece of work (see also p. 33).

7 Relate new information and ideas to things you already know

You will find it easiest to understand new things, and to remember them, if you have mastered the fundamentals of a subject and have a firm foundation on which to build. You can then try to link new material to familiar things in a meaningful sequence, or to fit them in as part of a pattern so that they come to be associated in your mind.

Each time you make additions to your notes on a new aspect of the course, therefore, look through your earlier work. This will help you to consider each week's work in relation to the course as a whole. You can fit in new material at appropriate points and add cross references to remind you of connections between current work and earlier work.

Recognising features common to different processes, or general principles that can be applied in novel situations, or rules that can be used in solving new problems, will all help you to select those things that you must learn and as a result there will be fewer things for you to try to remember.

It is also worth trying to view your studies of each subject in your course in the light of your increasing knowledge and understanding of other subjects. You will see unexpected as well as expected connections; and this will add interest to your studies and make learning easier.

8   Keep your previous work fresh in your mind

Do not concentrate solely on current work. Look at recent examination papers (those for last year and the year before), which should be similar to the examinations you will be taking. Solve problems and plan written answers to the questions, on work you have completed, to make sure that you can answer them. You will also find suitable test questions in appropriate chapters of your textbooks.

In answering questions you not only test yourself and refresh your memory but also bring together relevant information from different parts of your course, arrange it for a particular purpose, and so give yourself practice in preparing and answering the kinds of questions that you expect to be set in your examinations.

Different kinds of questions test different abilities, and using your knowledge to answer questions in course work, and in revision for your examinations, should help you to develop the necessary skills (see Table 9.1).

Overcoming difficulties and finding answers to your questions,

Table 9.1   Answering questions and developing your ability

Course work and homework	Practice in answering questions	Abilities tested in your answers to questions
Acquiring knowledge ——————→	RECALL ——————→	Ability to: REMEMBER
	↓	UNDERSTAND
Observing	SELECT ——————→	EXPLAIN
	↓	APPLY
Listening	ORGANISE	EVALUATE
	↓	ANALYSE
Reading	RE-ARRANGE ——————→	SYNTHESISE
	↓	REASON
Increasing your understanding	SOLVE PROBLEMS ——————→	PREDICT CALCULATE

as they arise, also makes you think again and look at your notes, consult appropriate reference books, or ask your teachers. In this way, incidentally, you revise as you extend your knowledge.

In using your knowledge you think repeatedly about your work: you *select* what is required in a complete answer to the question, you *consider* how the material should be arranged to make an effective answer, you *think* as you write, and you *think again* as you check the work. Thinking repeatedly (see p. 155) helps to fix relevant information and ideas in your mind.

Having to put your thoughts in order, for a particular purpose, makes you recognise the parts of your answer and put them together. The organisation and the association of ideas help you to commit them to memory and contribute to your better understanding of the subject. Sometimes things suddenly seem to fall into place. From then on you have no difficulty in completing similar tasks. Sometimes sleeping on a problem, or putting it on one side for a while before thinking again, may yield similar beneficial results.

9 Prepare special revision notes

When you are sure you understand an aspect of your work, select the points that you consider most important. Do not try to remember whole pages of writing (from your notes or from a textbook).

In course work your teachers will discourage copying from books, and in marking examination questions examiners will not expect or want you to remember extracts from your textbooks word for word. They prefer you to understand what you have read, select the most important points, remember these, and then convey your knowledge and understanding in your own words.

If you take good notes in class and amend them where necessary in your further studies, as suggested on page 32, your notes should contain all the information needed in your examinations. Indeed, they will probably contain more than you could remember in last-minute revision.

In earlier revision sessions, therefore, it is a good idea to study your notes carefully. In the light of your increasing knowledge of each subject, decide which are the most important points. Then underline them for emphasis or make comments in the margin to direct your attention.

During your course, especially at weekends and in the holidays when you are reviewing work done in the preceding weeks or months, study your notes carefully. Decide what are the most important aspects of your course, in relation to your preparations for taking tests and examinations, as indicated by the syllabus and by questions asked in course work, tests and examinations. Make sure you understand each aspect and then make very short revision notes.

It is a good idea to use an index card or postcard for each note. On one card, for example, you might include a rule that you wish to remember, a mnemonic to help you to remember (see p. 153), a poem, definition, chemical formula, or anything else that you intend to learn by heart, or carefully selected points that you wish to remember on one aspect of your work – such as a plan for a composition, a summary of a chapter in a book, a flow chart, or some other simple diagram.

Preparing revision notes, so that you reduce things that you know and understand to essentials, provides an opportunity to go over earlier work. Preparing and improving these notes provides definite tasks that can be fitted into thirty-minute study periods throughout your course, to aid concentration by making you think about one aspect of your work. Once prepared, looking at these short notes, to refresh your memory, provides smaller tasks that can be fitted into much shorter times which might be insufficient for other useful work. You may also find it helpful to read your revision notes aloud, and even to record them on tape so that you can play them back repeatedly (see p. 157). Memorising is aided by repetition, and by the use of more than one of the senses (e.g. hearing as well as seeing).

Selecting the essentials is an aid to learning, in itself, and you will remember more than the words written in these short revision notes. As a result, each time you look at them you are reminded of more than the essentials. Each word reminds you of other things observed by yourself, mentioned by your teachers, or read in books. Reducing your notes to essentials leaves you with less to remember, and yet you are able to remember more.

If prepared carefully, therefore, your own revision notes are a valuable study aid. They should be much more useful to you – at all stages in your studies – than could be similar notes prepared by anyone else.

10 Use memory cues sparingly

For learning by heart it is sometimes helpful to remember a mnemonic or memory cue. For example, those studying physics or painting – and anyone interested in rainbows – may remember the order of colours in a spectrum by memorising the mnemonic: *Richard of York gave battle in vain.* The initial letters of these words are the same as for the colours: red, orange, yellow, green, blue, indigo and violet.

In nautical language the right-hand side of a vessel, looking forward, is called the starboard side and is marked by a green light, whereas the left-hand side is called the port side and is marked by a red light. If you wished to remember this you might do so by repeating the words:

$\uparrow$ right
starboard
green

until they were fixed in your memory. Alternatively, you might note that the words *right*, *starboard* and *green* are all longer than
left   *port*   and *red*
and that the longer words go together, as do the shorter words. Having noted this you will remember *right*, *starboard* and *green* without further thought. However, it would add interest to your studies to read in a dictionary that boats used to be steered by a paddle placed over the right-hand side and that *starboard*, therefore, comes from *steer-board*. Wherever possible in study, it is better to understand things than to rely on the memory alone.

11 Space your revision

Do not study first, completing your course, in the belief that you can revise later. Revision should be part of study, from the start of your course, so that you have the maximum time in which to understand, select, learn and remember.

End each study period with a few minutes spent recalling the work you have been doing, and then revising (see p. 12 and 33). To help you do this, teachers may end a lesson and authors may end a chapter with a summary of the most important points they wish to draw to your attention.

Immediately after learning something for the first time you can probably remember most of what you have learnt, but your memory may soon fade if you do not think about this work again. Some psychologists find it useful to speak of a short-term memory, which soon fades. They *suggest* that revision helps to transfer things you wish to remember to a long-term memory.

After a study period you *may* forget quickly at first and then more slowly, and without revision you *might* eventually forget most of what you have learnt. In each revision period you certainly do not start at the beginning: furthermore, you refresh your memory quickly. That is to say, your second study period does not need to be as long as the first. In successive study periods, which may be more and more widely spaced, you refresh your memory quicker. And after each revision period you remember more – forget less! Note, however, that people differ in their ability to retain information – which depends so much upon their interest in the subject – and it is not easy to measure the amount remembered by any individual at any time.

So that you do not forget things once you have studied and understood them, and to keep all aspects of your work fresh in your mind, you are advised to space your revision throughout your course.

1 Soon after making notes in class or whilst reading, perhaps the same evening or the next day, try to look through them – marking the main points (as suggested on pp. 12 and 33).
2 Review each subject studied during the week, revising the main points, at the next weekend. Consider what you have learnt. This need not take long.
3 Revise each subject during the holidays, if you are taking a full-time course. This is especially important during the twelve months preceding an examination.
4 Revise each subject again, covering all aspects studied in your course, in your final revision period – in the six to eight weeks immediately before the examinations.

12 Devote short periods to revision
Most time in study should be devoted to thinking about your work and using your knowledge. One way to use your understanding of

any aspect of your work is in deciding what you need to know and then preparing revision notes. You can then study these notes carefully later, knowing that you are concentrating on essentials; but so that you can concentrate most effectively do not study them for long at any one time.

To sit trying to cram information into your brain, for long periods, is likely to be both tedious and unrewarding. This is another reason why it is a mistake to leave all your revision until the last few weeks of your course. It is better to select a few things that you wish to remember and then pay attention to these, rather than try to learn too much at one time.

This is why a teacher, planning a lesson, does not try to convey too many new ideas or too much information in any one class. Knowing that your concentration will be greatest when you begin any task, a teacher may devote different parts of a forty-minute lesson to different activities. For example, a teacher may spend:

15   minutes explaining three or four things that you should try to understand;
15   minutes allowing you to practise a skill or testing that you have remembered and understood; and then
10   minutes answering your questions and revising, in an attempt to ensure that you have understood and will remember.

In a lesson planned in this way you will be able to concentrate on one task at the beginning – listening and noting the main points. You maintain your concentration by starting upon a new task, set by the teacher to occupy the middle part of the lesson; and you can concentrate again on the third task, in which you are reminded of the main points made during the lesson.

13   Repeat things you wish to remember

You may never forget the words of a popular song, even though you did not consciously try to remember them, because they captured your attention, you enjoyed listening to the song, and you heard it repeatedly. These are three basic requirements for the learner: attention, interest and repetition (see Table 9.2).

Thinking again and again about any subject helps to fix things in your mind. This is another reason why a good teacher may (*a*) start a

Table 9.2 Basic requirements for learning and remembering

Interest	1	Work to some purpose.
	2	Study things you find interesting and develop your interest.
Attention	3	Survey the whole before studying its parts.
	4	Get things right the first time.
	5	Concentrate on one task at a time.
Association	6	Keep your notes in good order.
	7	Relate new information and ideas to things you already know.
	8	Use your knowledge.
Selection	9	Make sure you understand and then prepare very short revision notes, flow charts, etc.
	10	Use memory cues sparingly.
Repetition	11	Space your revision.
	12	Devote short periods to revision.
	13	Repeat and remember.

lesson with an outline of the ground to be covered, (*b*) continue by emphasising a few points, then (*c*) make you use this information, and (*d*) end with a summary which includes the main points yet again.

Similarly, in a textbook for an introductory course, each chapter may begin with an outline of what the chapter is to be about, then emphasise the main points by headings, effective paragraphing, and the use of **bold** and *italic* print, and then end with a summary. Questions at the end of the chapter, like the questions asked at the end of a lesson, also serve to make you think again. They help to test your understanding and help you to remember, and so they are an aid to learning.

Repetition also results in your private studies from spacing your revision (as recommended on p. 153), from linking new work with things you already know (see p. 149), from using your knowledge of each subject (see p. 150) and from preparing revision notes (see p. 151). Then in each short period of revision (see p. 154), you can allow important thoughts – selected previously – to pass through your mind.

The importance of repetition is obvious in learning a new language. Indeed, children learn their own language by hearing words again and again, associating them with objects and emotions and with other words in different contexts. In learning a language, repetition in hearing and saying words aloud helps to fix the words, their meaning and their pronunciation in your mind. You may listen to the sounds of words in tape recordings, practise using words in conversation with friends, and use words during visits to countries where the language is spoken.

For anything you wish to learn by heart, the best way is to devote short periods to the task and to distribute them over as long a time as possible.

To help with your revision, for example in vacations and before examinations, the cards used for your revision notes can be kept in a card index. Each card can be marked 2, 4, 8, 16 and 32, and the index can be divided according to the days of the month. A card can then be placed for attention on a particular day so that it can be studied carefully, but for a short time, on one day, and then two days later, four days later, and so on, during the weeks you have planned to devote to revision.

The cards you intend to study on one day can also be kept in your pocket. You can look through them several times during that day in the odd moments available for revision, from time to time, that would not be long enough for other study tasks.

Rules for revising

It should be possible to answer all questions set in course work, tests and examinations, in an introductory course, from the ideas and information included in the textbook recommended for the course. Throughout the course, therefore, you must devote enough time to reading your textbooks (see p. 19), reflecting on your class notes in the light of your further studies (see p. 50), and preparing special revision notes (see p. 151).

1   Revise as a regular part of study
Being well organised, so that you work steadily throughout the course with revision as part of active study (as recommended on pp. 12 and 33), will help you to avoid the last-minute overwork or panic that prevents some students from doing their best work in tests and examinations.

However, in the last year before examinations your revision must be planned so that, in addition to coping with current work, you can go over all relevant aspects of each subject several times.

2   Prepare a timetable or schedule for your final revision

In the last eight weeks or so immediately before your examinations, revise the most important points again and again from your revision notes (see p. 151). In doing this final revision you should not be trying to learn new things, in an attempt to make up for lost time. You should simply be refreshing your memory.

Prepare a plan for the final six to eight weeks of your revision, allowing yourself enough time to revise all aspects of your work again (see p. 50). Begin revising each subject at the start of this final revision period. Do not revise one subject at a time or you may run out of time and find that you cannot revise some subjects at all. It is better to be able to answer most of the questions on all of your examination papers than to be able to answer all the questions on most of the papers but not enough on some.

In this final revision period, set yourself target dates or deadlines by which you will complete each part of your revision of the material upon which you will be tested in your examinations, so that you have objectives each day, as well as each week, and can complete your revision before the dates fixed for examinations.

If there are classes during this final revision period it is important to attend: the teacher will probably be drawing aspects of the work together and coming to conclusions. If your revision has been well organised, throughout your course, you will not be tempted to miss these classes and you will be well placed to derive maximum benefit from them.

If you have fewer classes, or no classes, in the weeks just before an examination, you may have more time than previously for private study. If you can, it is a good idea to get into the habit of thinking and writing about your work in study periods that correspond to the times at which you will have to work in your examinations (for example, from 9.30 to 12.30 and from 13.30 to 16.30 hours), so that you can get used to concentrating and working effectively for two or three hours, as necessary, without a break.

Also, in your revision schedule, include enough time for sleep (eight hours each night), regular breaks for recreation, and occasional days off work. The result of working too hard, and of not having enough sleep, or enough exercise and other forms of recreation, is under-achievement in examinations. Overwork results in tiredness at the very time when you would like to be at your best; and recreation and rest should result in physical and mental refreshment.

3   Learn from last year's question papers

Look at last year's examination papers for each of the subjects you will be taking. Read the instructions at the head of each paper, which tell you (*a*) how much time is allowed; (*b*) how many questions have to be answered in this time; (*c*) whether all the questions have to be answered or if there is a choice; (*d*) if there is a choice, how many questions must be answered; and (*e*) if there are any restrictions on your choice.

Candidates who do not answer enough questions lose opportunities to score marks; and those who answer too many questions cannot score extra marks because the extra questions they answer will not be marked. Similarly, it is not possible to compensate for not answering a compulsory question by answering an extra question on another part of the paper. These are some of the ways in which candidates lose opportunities to score marks by not obeying the instructions at the head of the paper.

Look to see the kinds of questions set, how they are laid out, and how the questions are arranged (as discussed in Part Two of this book). Note also the aspects of each subject tested on each paper. Look at each question and consider what the examiner wanted to know. Why is each word in the question needed? Plan answers to the questions.

You may find it useful to look at examination papers for two years ago, as well as at last year's papers. Some people try to 'spot' questions, after noting that a question on a particular topic seems to be set in most years or that a question on another topic has not been set recently and thinking that one may be set this year. Such question-spotting can be no more than a guide to what you may be asked, even if questions are set regularly on a certain topic, because these questions are not usually identical. A slight change in the wording can make a great deal of difference to what is required in a sensible answer (see p. 172). If you prepare an answer during your revision, therefore, it is essential that you read any question carefully *in the examination* before you decide to answer it. Then prepare an answer to precisely the question asked.

Learning specimen answers (or so-called model answers) prepared by other people, without understanding, is not recommended as a method of preparing for examinations. Similarly, books of revision notes prepared by teachers whose courses you have not attended are bound to be an inadequate substitute for your own teacher or textbook supported by revision notes you have prepared yourself. Your own notes will remind you of background information that is not recorded in the notes. It is necessary to have understood the course before you can understand revision notes that provide a skeleton but no flesh. There is of course a market for books of revision notes, as there is for quack remedies: there will always be students who are on the look out for a magic formula that will take the work out of study. And because concise notes prepared by someone else are likely to be of little use to you, some books sold as revision aids contain much more than the minimum amount of information. They are textbooks under another name. Evaluate these, as you would any other textbooks (see p. 16), to see if you think you might find them helpful.

4   Practise answering questions
In addition to planning answers to essay-type questions, it is important to practise planning and answering all types of questions in the time that would be available for them in an examination. This is a useful exercise, to be completed from time to time during your course, but it is especially important to have such practice in the weeks preceding your examinations. Otherwise you may find yourself capable of answering enough questions in the examination, but be unable to do so because you have not developed the ability to first allocate your time and then complete each answer in the limited time available. In the answer to each question the examiner is looking for quality, not quantity, and a good answer to each question can be completed in the time the examiners have allowed for it.

5   Tackle last year's papers

As well as answering isolated questions in a fixed time, from start to finish, it is important to give yourself practice in completing the number of questions that must be answered in the examination in the time that will be available. The best way to do this is to ensure that you will not be disturbed and then tackle some of last year's papers as mock examinations, in the time stated on each paper, during the weeks preceding your examinations. You should not find this too difficult because you will probably have answered, or planned answers, to individual questions previously.

It is a good idea to read the Examiners' report on last year's examinations, which you should be able to purchase from the examinations authority if it is not in your school or college library. This report will probably not contain the questions, but if you have the question papers and your own answers you can learn from the examiners' comments on how last year's candidates tackled each question – including notes on common mistakes or misunderstandings.

Also, if you have taken mock examinations at school or college, for practice as part of your preparation for your final examinations, it is important to assess your performance critically. For example: (1) did you allocate your time sensibly, so that you could spend enough but not too much time on each question; and (2) did you just write all you know in any answer, instead of answering the question? Many students do not do as well as they might in examinations because they do not allocate their time according to the marks available for each question, and they do not answer precisely the question asked. These are the two most common faults in examination technique.

As with assessed course work, if your answer papers are returned to you, with your teachers' marks and comments, try to learn from any corrections so that you do not make the same mistakes again. Consider any advice. Can you improve your examination technique?

A poor mark in a mock examination may cause you to start working harder, and an average mark may make you determined to do better. But if you do well in these examinations this is not a reason for complacency. Keep on studying and using effective revision techniques so that in the examinations you can do your best work.

Summary

Rules for learning
1   Know *why* you wish to learn.
2   Study things you find interesting.
3   Survey the whole before you study its parts.
4   Get things right the first time.
5   Concentrate on one task at a time.
6   Keep your notes on each subject in good order.
7   Relate new information and ideas to things you already know.
8   Keep your previous work fresh in your mind.
9   Prepare special revision notes.
10   Use memory cues sparingly.
11   Space your revision.
12   Devote short periods to revision.
13   Repeat things you wish to remember.

Rules for revising
1   Revise as a regular part of study.
2   Prepare a timetable or schedule for your final revision.
3   Learn from last year's question papers.
4   Practise answering questions.
5   Tackle last year's paper.

10

Taking Tests and Examinations

This chapter will help you, after working effectively from the start of your course, to display your knowledge and understanding in progress tests and examinations, and to achieve grades that are a true indication of your ability in the examinations at the end of your course.

Final preparations for tests and examinations

As soon as the dates of your tests and examinations are known, include them in your plan for the final weeks of your revision. Find out where each test or examination is to be held and add this information to your plan.

Consider what materials you will need in each examination, including reference materials, if any, that you will be allowed to use. Make sure that you have these things and that they are in good order. For example, make sure that the batteries of your calculator are fully charged.

On the day before any test or examination, check that you have noted the time and place correctly. Put together the clothes you intend to wear, the equipment you will need in the examination, and anything you will need on your journey. Try to get eight hours' sleep, and make arrangements to ensure that you get out of bed at the right time. Give yourself time for a light meal, and for your journey, so that you can relax before the examination. If you are well prepared you need not be over anxious, but you do not want to be worried that you might not arrive on time.

Do not talk to other candidates about the examination, either on your way to the examination or while you are waiting to enter the room. It is best, if you can, to keep to yourself at this time or talk to someone who is not involved in this examination.

Go to the lavatory. Then, if possible, enter the examination room before the starting time, so that you can arrange any papers or equipment that you are allowed to use on your working surface. You can also write the personal details required on the front cover of your answer book, as soon as you are told that you may do so.

Scoring marks in tests

Read the instructions at the beginning of the test paper. Then, if anything is unclear, explain your difficulty to the invigilator, who may clarify the point.

Tests during a course are usually made up of the kinds of questions considered in Chapters 5 and 6. Also, some examinations comprise only questions of this type. In such tests and examinations you will probably be asked to attempt all the questions.

The time allowed for the whole paper will be stated at the beginning, immediately below the heading. If the paper is in parts, you may be told how many questions must be answered from each part and advised how to allocate your time between the parts. For example, if the paper is in three parts:

> *Part 1*   50 multiple choice questions;
> *Part 2*   30 true or false questions; and
> *Part 3*   5 essay-type questions;

you may be told to answer all questions in *Parts 1 and 2* and any two questions from Part 3, and advised to spend one hour on each part (in a three-hour examination).

In objective test questions your answer to each question will be either right or wrong: you score either full marks for a correct answer or no marks for an incorrect answer.

The instructions at the head of the paper, or in each question, will state how your answers are to be recorded. For example, you may be instructed to underline the answer you think is correct, to mark the correct answer by a tick in a space provided, to draw a circle round the letter of your choice, to write 'true' or 'false' next to each of a number of statements, or to mark your answers in a particular way on separate answer sheets. *You must follow these instructions exactly*.

Make sure you indicate your choice of answer carefully and neatly, so that your decision is clear to the person marking your work.

In tests made up of short-answer questions, if you have to attempt all the questions, it is not necessary to read through the whole paper before starting your answers. Indeed, to do so would be a waste of time. It is also a mistake to work slowly through the paper, once only, answering both the easy and more difficult questions as you come to them. If you did this you would be held up by any questions you found difficult and the result might be that you had no time left in which to attempt some questions towards the end of the paper.

Tackle test papers this way

1 Start with question 1 and work through the paper, reading each question carefully and answering those you find easy: the ones you are confident you can answer correctly.

2 Think about each question for a few moments to make sure that you have understood what is required; then give a considered answer. Make a tick in the left-hand margin, next to the question, to indicate to yourself later that you have completed this question.

3 If you are not certain of the correct answer to any question, put a question mark in the left-hand margin, next to the question, to remind you to come back to this question later if you have time. If you wish, make notes in the margin for your later consideration.

4 Pass on to the next question. Do not spend time, on first reading through the paper, pondering on questions you find difficult. If you do allow yourself to get bogged down on questions you find difficult, this may cause you to run out of time – and to miss the opportunity to look at the last questions, some of which you might have found easy. Remember, in a test made up of short-answer questions, that you will probably score as many marks for answering the questions you find easy as for answering those that you find difficult. Therefore, be sure to answer the easy questions.

5   When you have answered all the questions you find easy, work through the paper a second time, tackling the remaining questions. On re-reading some of the questions you at first found difficult, the answer may come to mind. As you answer them, put a tick in the margin next to or through the question mark you placed there earlier as a reminder.

6   Write a second question mark in the margin next to any question you still cannot answer.

7   If at all possible, allow time to read all the questions a third time – checking each answer carefully but not changing any answer at this stage unless you are sure that you are correcting a mistake. Think yet again about any question that is still un-answered, to see if you can add to your score.

If you are not sure of the answer, should you guess?

Below the heading of the question paper there may be a statement that marks will be deducted for each incorrect answer. However, if your guess is based on your knowledge of the subject you are more likely to be right than wrong.

Remember also that in true or false questions you are as likely to get the answer right as wrong – just by chance. You would expect to gain a mark about as often as you lost a mark, therefore, even if you knew nothing about the subject.

In tackling multiple choice questions, in which you have to pick one answer from either four or five, your chances of getting the correct answer just by chance will be one in four or one in five respectively. That is to say, if you have no idea which is the correct answer, your guess is more likely to be wrong than right.

In true or false questions, if you are not sure of the answer, always make a considered guess. In multiple choice, multiple response and matching pair questions it is probably best not to guess unless you have eliminated some possibilities and are fairly confident that your guess will be right. However, unless you are told in any test that marks will be deducted for wrong answers, you have nothing to lose by guessing: you should answer *all* the questions, so that you can score marks not only for those you know are right but also for those that happen to be right.

If the examiners apply a correction to ensure that a candidate's marks are not increased as a result of uninformed guessing, that correction is related to the chances of getting answers right just by chance. The poor candidate, therefore, should neither gain nor lose marks on the paper as a whole, as a result of guessing, but the informed guesses of good students should result in their gaining marks.

When you come to tackle objective tests and examinations, think about each question in relation to the course of study you have just completed, and the syllabus and textbook for the course, so that the question is considered in an appropriate context. This is especially important if the test papers are set and marked by your own teachers. The questions set, and the answers expected, will be based on the course they have planned and taught.

Objective tests are useful for teachers because they can be included in a course as a means of assessing the progress of all students taking that course – on each aspect of the syllabus, and to recognise any aspect of the work that individual students are finding difficult.

Objective tests are useful to both teachers and examiners because they are easy to mark and – because all questions must be answered and there is a definite answer to each question – the results of all candidates are directly comparable.

However, one disadvantage of their use in assessment is that some of the false statements may not be recognised as such. Incorrect answers, if remembered, may then stand in the way of learning. After answering objective test questions, therefore, it is a good idea to check your class notes and your textbook if you are uncertain of the answer to any question. Make sure that the answer fixed in your mind is correct.

It is helpful if teachers discuss the questions with all members of a class, after an objective test, to ensure that each student understands not only which option(s) is/are correct, but also why the others – though plausible – are incorrect. This will help to avoid misunderstandings and will be an aid to learning.

Objective tests can be used to assess certain abilities (for example, the ability to remember, to understand, to analyse and to interpret), but to test a student's originality, or ability in written expression, for example, other kinds of question must be set. This is why, in many subjects, students are assessed in other ways – as well as, or instead of, by objective tests.

Scoring marks in written examinations

Your success in tests and written examinations depends upon:

1   effective study throughout your course, to increase your knowledge and understanding of the subject;
2   well planned revision;
3   practice in planning and answering the kinds of questions set in tests and examinations;
4   reading and obeying any instructions given at the beginning of each test or examination paper;
5   your ability to read and interpret questions correctly; and
6   your effective use of time during each test and examination, so that you (*a*) choose questions wisely, (*b*) answer the required number of questions, (*c*) write legibly and arrange your answers effectively, and (*d*) convey your knowledge and understanding to the best of your ability.

Fill in details on the front of your answer book
Before a test or examination starts, you will be given time to enter the information asked for on the answer sheet or on the front page of your answer book, such as:

1   your name, written in capital letters;
2   the number of the centre at which you are taking the test or examination;
3   the name of the subject you are taking (copied from the heading of the question paper); and
4   the date.

Read any instructions on the front of the answer book. For example, do you have to start each question at the top of a page? Read and obey any instructions of this kind.

Read all the instructions at the head of the question paper
Have you been given the right paper?
Do you have to answer all the questions?
If not, how many questions have you to answer?
Is there any restriction on your choice of questions? For example, is there a compulsory question? Do you have to answer at least one question from each section?

How much time do you have in which to complete the whole examination?

Is any advice given about how to allocate your time? For example, if the paper is in three parts and it is a three-hour examination, you may be advised to spend an hour on each part. This would mean that one-third of the marks available for the whole paper will be allocated to each part.

Survey the whole paper quickly

Glance through your paper. Is it complete and properly printed?

Is it divided into sections?

Are there questions on both sides of each page?

How are the questions arranged?

What kinds of questions have been set?

The paper should be similar to last year's paper in the arrangement of questions and in the kinds of questions set. You should, therefore, be on familiar ground. Looking at last year's papers during your revision (see p. 159) should help you to settle down quickly during your own examination.

Read all the questions carefully before deciding which ones you will answer

Unless you are asked to answer all the questions on the paper, you must read every question carefully before you can decide which ones you can answer best.

1 If the paper is divided into sections, select questions according to the instructions at the head of the paper so that you do tackle any compulsory questions and you do attempt the required number of questions from each section.

2 Select the questions that you can answer best. These will usually be the ones you can answer most completely: if possible, you must answer all parts of every question you attempt. They will usually also be the questions which, for you, are the easiest. Do not attempt what seem to you to be the most difficult questions, just to show how clever you are.

3 Allocate your time according to the marks available for each question. If the questions carry equal marks, divide the time available for the whole examination by the number of questions

you must answer – remembering that you will need to allow time for reading the whole paper and selecting questions at the beginning and for checking your work at the end.

4 Answer the question you expect to find easiest first, but do not spend more time on this question just because you think you can answer it best.

5 Answer the easiest questions first and end with the one you expect to find most difficult.

6 However, you must answer any compulsory question. You may like to start with this, knowing that you must attempt it, so that you can either get it out of the way or make a start and come back to it later (*a*) if you are unable to complete it at the first attempt and (*b*) if you have time to spare after doing the other questions.

Read each question again immediately before starting your answer

To answer any question, in a test or examination – or at any other time – you must understand every word in the question and appreciate exactly what is required in your answer (see p. 112). Every question, therefore, tests your general vocabulary as well as your knowledge of a particular subject.

Remember, also, that some questions contain information that you will need, or that will help you, to work out your answer. This is obviously true in calculations. It is also true, especially, in questions that ask you to comment on unfamiliar material.

Also, there are some questions (such as comprehension questions, see p. 108) in which all the information needed for your answer is given in the question. You are asked to read a passage carefully and then answer questions that test your understanding of the passage.

Write the question number in the left-hand margin of your answer book

This number indicates where your answer starts. *Do not waste time in copying out the question.*

If the question is set in parts, indicate the start of each part of your answer, so that your work is easy to mark.

For example:

From the words of this question, give an example of (*a*) a verb, (*b*) a noun, and (*c*) a conjunction.

If this were question 1 on the paper you would write the number **1** in the margin at the start of your answer and then use the letters *a*, *b* and *c* to indicate the parts of your answer, corresponding to the parts of the question.

Specimen answer

1	(*a*)	give
	(*b*)	example
	(*c*)	and

Note: See page 94 for definitions of the parts of your speech.

Similarly, if asked to use certain headings you must do so, and it is usually best to use them in the same order as they appear in the question. They signpost the parts of your answer, and this is the order in which the examiner is expecting to mark these parts.

In answering each question, do as much as you are asked but no more

In any question, if you are asked to give **one** reason, do not waste your time by giving more than one. Just give one reason that you are sure is correct.

If you give additional reasons, some of which are incorrect, you may score no marks because the examiner may assume you do not know which of the answers you have given are correct. Remember, also, that if full marks are to be scored for one correct reason, you will not be able to score more marks by giving extra reasons – even if they are all correct.

For example:

Name *one* punctuation mark that may be used to indicate the end of a sentence.

If this were question 2 on the paper you would write the number **2** in the margin and then your answer.

Specimen answer

| 2 | A full stop |

Note that other correct answers to this question would be:
    either   A question mark
     or   An exclamation mark
but if you are asked to name *one* do not name more than one.

Similarly, if asked to do **either** one thing **or** another, do not do both.

If asked to *include* a labelled diagram in your answer you must do so. But if asked to *answer by means of* a labelled diagram, **only** the labelled diagram is required – no more.

Always answer the question, the whole question, but no more!

Think before you answer
In problem solving and calculations, think and then calculate. Show each step in your calculations, because marks are given for the knowledge displayed in your working towards your answer, as well as for the correct answer.

Similarly, in written answers when a sentence, paragraph or a longer composition is required, always think before writing – as you would in course work. Because time is limited in tests and examinations you may be tempted to use all the time in writing, but some time devoted to thinking and planning before you write should result in your using the remaining time more effectively – so that you will probably score more marks than would otherwise have been possible (see p. 132).

Planning is even more necessary in examinations than in course work, because you have no spare time for re-writing badly organised, incomplete or otherwise unsatisfactory answers.

If you have planned an answer to a question in your revision, similar to the answer that seems to be required to a question set in your examination, it is especially important to think again and to plan your examination answer – to take account of even a slight difference in the wording of the question, which might make a great deal of difference to the answer required. In battle, the signal 'The troops will not advance' means the opposite of the signal 'The troops will now advance'. Only one letter is different, but a very different response is required!

When you start writing, keep to your plan. This should help you to get to the point quickly, to answer all parts of the question, to arrange these parts in an effective order (for easy reading and easy marking), and to include all that is necessary to score full marks in the time available.

For further advice on preparing effective answers to different types of questions, see Part Two of this book (Chapters 5 to 8).

Answer as many questions as are required but no more
Allocate your time to each question according to the proportion of the total marks available for the question, and the time available for all your answers.

If you are asked to answer five questions there will usually be twenty marks for each one. So if you answer only four questions, you will be marked out of eighty instead of a hundred. It is important to allocate your time sensibly and to answer five ques-

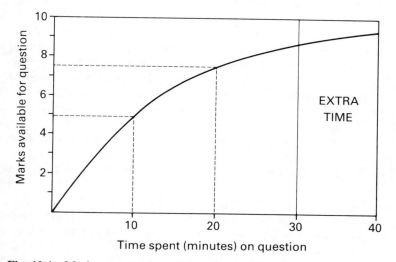

Fig. 10.1 Marks scored for a written answer related to the time spent on the composition: it is easy to score some marks for most questions but difficult to score full marks for any question

tions even if you cannot write a good answer to the last one. Remember that it is always easier to get a few marks for a question, even if you do not know much about it, than to score extra marks for another question on which you have already spent long enough (see Fig. 10.1).

If because of bad timing you are short of time for your last question, answer it in note form. A plan of your answer is much better than no answer at all. Credit will be given for relevant material displayed in this way.

Check your work

When you allocate time at the beginning of an examination, remember to leave time for reading through every answer at the end – to check your work. Delete any rough work; correct any slips of the pen, and add relevant details that you did not remember previously. In this way you may (*a*) prevent yourself from losing marks and (*b*) score extra marks. Time spent in checking your work is therefore well spent.

Check that every number and letter is legible (see p. 60). Remember that it is not possible to score marks for anything that cannot be read.

Also check that your answers read well. In most examinations credit is given for good English. Examiners may give credit directly, by awarding marks for good English – as in an examination in English Language or English Literature. Or marks may be gained indirectly because good English is clear and direct, and this helps the examiner to read and understand the work easily, and to give credit where credit is due.

Inevitably, if paragraphs are in an ineffective order, if sentences are poorly constructed with faults in punctuation and grammar, or if words are spelt incorrectly, your meaning is unlikely to be clear and marks will be lost.

Never leave an examination before the end. If there is time, go over your work again to see if it is possible to add any relevant point that may score you a few more marks. They may raise your result for the examination from a fail to a pass, or from one grade to the next.

After the examination

1 Avoid discussing the examination questions with other candidates. They are unlikely to agree about what is required in each answer and their opinions may cause you unnecessary alarm.
2 Relax for a while, doing something completely different.
3 Prepare for your next examination paper.

Books for Reference and Further Reading

For homework, always have your class notes and your textbook for the subject with you for reference or close study. Have a dictionary to hand whenever you study. For first examinations a small dictionary will suffice for most subjects, for example: *Chambers' New Compact Dictionary* (Chambers, Edinburgh); *Collins' Pocket Dictionary of the English Language* (Collins, Glasgow); or *The Pocket Oxford Dictionary* (Clarendon Press, Oxford). However, if you intend to go on to more advanced studies you will be handicapped unnecessarily if you do not have a larger dictionary, for example: *Chambers' Twentieth Century Dictionary* (Chambers, Edinburgh); *Collins' Concise Dictionary of The English Language* (Collins', Glasgow); *The Concise Oxford Dictionary* (Clarendon Press, Oxford); *Longman Modern English Dictionary* (Longman, London); or, for American English, *Webster's New Collegiate Dictionary* (Merriam, Mass.).

This book on *Study and Examination Techniques* is in the Teach Yourself series (Hodder & Stoughton, Sevenoaks). Other books in this series, for students of all subjects, include Phythian, B. A. (1980) *English Grammar*; Phythian, B. A. (1985) *Good English*; Thornhill, P. (1983) *Spelling*; and Sassoon, R. & Briem, G. SE (1984) *Handwriting*.

Students taking advanced courses will find further advice and guidance on writing as part of study, and on study, revision and examination techniques, in the handbooks:

Barrass, R. (1982) *Students Must Write: A guide to better writing in course work and examinations* (Methuen, London);

Barrass, R. (1984) *Study! A guide to effective study, revision and examination techniques* (Chapman & Hall, London);

Gowers, E. (1973) *The Complete Plain Words*, 2nd edn, revised by Sir Bruce Fraser (HMSO, London).

Index